Part
Using Asse

Contents

Description of the Assessments T2

Principles of Assessment T3

Assessment: Questions and Answers T4

Administering Assessments T5

Scoring T6

Self-Assessment Checklist T9

Peer Assessment Checklist T10

Group Assessment Chart T11

Class Summary Chart T12

INTRODUCTION

This Assessment Book includes information about assessment in McGraw-Hill's **Adventures in Time and Place,** directions for administering and scoring Chapter Tests, Unit Tests, and Performance Assessments, blackline masters, and answer keys.

Description of the Assessments

There are two types of assessments provided in this book for *Regions*: paper-and-pencil Chapter Tests and Unit Tests, and Performance Assessments for each chapter and unit.

Part 3 has **Chapter Test** blackline masters for each chapter in *Regions* and **Unit Test** blackline masters for each unit. Each Chapter Test comprises three sections:

- The **Content** section has 10 test questions, or items, about the content of the chapter. Five of the items are multiple-choice questions and five are short-answer questions — fill-in, matching, written response.

- The **Skills** section has 5 short-answer items for each skill taught in the chapter.

- The **Writing** section has two essay questions measuring both the content and skills in the chapter. The essay questions include a visual stimulus and require the student to write a brief paragraph.

Each Unit Test comprises two sections: a **Content and Skills** section with 10 multiple-choice items and 10 short-answer items measuring the content and skills taught in all of the chapters in the unit, and a **Writing** section with two essay questions measuring both the content and skills in the unit.

Answer Keys for all Chapter Tests and Unit Tests appear in sequence in Part 2.

Part 4 provides **Performance Assessments** for each chapter and each unit in *Regions*. There are three Chapter Performance Assessments in each chapter, based on the three *Think and Write* activities in the Chapter Review of the Pupil's Edition. Each of these activities results in a piece of writing, such as a journal entry or a letter.

Each Unit Performance Assessment is based on the Unit Project in the Unit Review of the Pupil's Edition. Each unit project results in a product that can be assessed. It also involves a process that can be evaluated through observation.

Each Performance Assessment provides guidelines for using the assessment. It includes the following:

- A statement of the **goal** of the activity or project

- **Suggestions** for modeling and instruction that will enable students to complete the activity or project

- **Portfolio Opportunities** that provide suggestions for evaluating student performance—including self-assessment and peer assessment—and incorporating the assessment into a portfolio

- A **Scoring Rubric** designed to help teachers evaluate each student's performance and score it as Excellent, Good, Fair, Poor, or Unscorable

Principles of Assessment

Assessment in **Adventures in Time and Place** involves the use of multiple measures in a wide variety of authentic situations to evaluate what students can do. Information collected through various forms of assessment is used for evaluation or making judgments about student performance. Forms of assessment provided with this program include both paper-and-pencil tests and performance assessments. Our approach to assessment is based on the following principles.

Assessment should be closely integrated with instruction.
It should be based on the goals of instruction, and it should measure what is taught, in the way in which it is taught.

Assessment should be based on the notion of *progress*—evaluating student progress toward achieving the goals and objectives of instruction.
It should be based on the ability to apply critical thinking strategies in a variety of contexts, not only on mastering isolated skills.

Assessment should be continuous, throughout the school year, and should incorporate a wide variety of modes and types of assessment.
Frequent assessments will provide formative information that is useful in guiding instruction. A wide variety of assessments will provide a comprehensive profile of each student.

Assessment tasks and activities should be direct and authentic, reflecting what students actually need to be able to do.
Assessment in authentic situations requires real-life tasks, which may involve any number of activities, from everyday classroom observations to student work samples to independent projects.

Authentic assessment activities should integrate social studies curriculum with all of the language arts: reading, writing, listening, speaking, and viewing.
Language arts are integrated in every aspect of real life, and they should be integrated in the classroom.

Assessment should include self-assessment and cooperative efforts between teacher and students, among student peers, and involving parents.
Students can learn a great deal from understanding and applying the standards of good work to their own achievements.

The assessments provided with this program are based on these principles of assessment. The Chapter Tests, Unit Tests, and Performance Assessments are intended to be administered at the end of each chapter and each unit. They are designed to help you determine how well students have mastered the content of the chapter or unit and how well they can apply the skills taught in the chapter or unit. Other ways of using tests, performance assessments, and portfolios with this program are described on the next page.

Assessment: Questions and Answers

Can the Chapter Tests be used in different ways?
Yes. The Chapter Tests have three sections: Content, Skills, and Writing. You may choose to give any or all of these sections when you administer the test, and you may use the sections of the test in other ways. For example, you might decide to use the Content section as a test and the Skills and Writing sections for instructional practice or follow-up instruction.

How can I use performance assessments with this program?
There are three general approaches to using performance assessment with this program. First, you can observe students in the classroom—during everyday activities and in specific activities outlined in the Teacher's Edition. Second, you can administer the Performance Assessments for each chapter and unit. Third, you can use portfolios.

How do I use the Performance Assessments?
When you have completed a chapter or unit, use the Performance Assessment guidelines in Part 4 to help prepare students to complete the activity or project and evaluate their performance. Each Performance Assessment offers suggestions for introducing the activity or project and assisting students in its completion, suggestions for using the assessment as a portfolio opportunity, and a scoring rubric for evaluating student performance.

What is portfolio assessment?
Simply stated, a portfolio is an organized collection of a student's work. A portfolio system can be as simple as a set of folders and a box to keep them in, but portfolio assessment is much more than that: it is a powerful concept for developing a comprehensive profile of each student.

How do I get started with portfolios?
Start with something simple and easy to manage. Introduce portfolios to the students as a way to organize their work. Tell them that they will be choosing their best works to put into the portfolio. At the beginning of the year, you may want to model the process by showing them your own portfolio or inviting guests, such as artists or photographers, to come in and show students their portfolios.

How do I involve students in portfolios?
Involving students is a critical part of portfolio assessment. Tell students they are responsible for taking care of their own portfolios. Talk with students to set goals for each unit and for the year. Work with them to choose their best works to help them meet their goals. Have students evaluate their own works by writing notes or completing self-assessments for each work they put into the portfolio. Periodically, have a portfolio review conference with students to look at what they have done, help them assess their own progress, and set new goals for the next unit.

How can I figure out students' grades from these assessment materials?
The tests are designed to be scored by section, and the score for each section can be converted to a percentage score for grading purposes. For the Writing section of each test and for the Performance Assessments, the student's performance can be scored on a 4-point scale. This type of score can also be converted to a percentage score for grading, as explained in the following pages.

Administering Assessments

The Chapter Tests, Unit Tests, and Performance Assessments are designed to be used with each chapter and unit. Before administering these assessments, familiarize yourself with the assessments themselves and the guidelines in this Teacher's Manual.

Administering Chapter and Unit Tests

The **Chapter Tests** and **Unit Tests** in Part 3 are designed for group administration. You may choose to administer the complete test or any of its parts.

These tests are not intended to be timed. Students should be given ample time to complete the tests. However, for planning purposes, the chart below shows the estimated time required to administer the sections of each kind of test.

Section	Number of Items	Estimated Time
Chapter Test		
Content	10	10–15 minutes
Skills	5 or 10	10–15 minutes
Writing	2 prompts	20–30 minutes
Unit Test		
Content and Skills	20	20–30 minutes
Writing	2 prompts	20–30 minutes

Depending on the needs of your students, you may decide to administer the entire test in one sitting, or you may administer sections of the test in separate sittings.

To administer a test, give a copy of the test to each student. Have students write their names at the top of each page. Directions for students appear at the top of each page. Have students read the directions, read the questions, and mark or write their answers on the test pages.

For multiple-choice items, students fill in the circle before the correct answer to each item. For short-answer questions, students write a letter, a word, a phrase, or a sentence on the lines provided. For each Writing prompt, students write a brief paragraph on the lines provided.

During the administration, check to see that each student is following the directions, is answering the right items, and is marking responses correctly.

Administering Performance Assessments

In Part 4 of this manual, you will find **Performance Assessments** for each chapter and each unit in *Regions*. Each Performance Assessment is one page intended for the teacher's use. The Chapter Performance Assessments are based on the Think and Write activities in the Chapter Review, and the Performance Assessment for each unit is based on the Unit Project in the Unit Review.

The Performance Assessments work in tandem with the Think and Write activities or Unit Projects to provide both instruction and assessment. When you have completed a chapter or unit, use the Performance Assessments to help prepare students to complete the Think and Write activity or Unit Project and then to evaluate their performance.

First, explain to students what they will be doing in the activity or project.

Second, use the suggestions at the top of the Performance Assessment page to introduce the activity or project and review instructional material from the chapter or unit.

Third, explain to students what is expected of them and how their work will be evaluated through the Performance Assessment.

Scoring

The Chapter Tests and Unit Tests are designed to be scored by section. Chapter Tests have three sections (Content, Skills, Writing) and Unit Tests have two sections (Content and Skills, Writing). For each test the correct responses are listed in the Answer Key (found in Part 2 of this manual).

For multiple-choice questions, the letter of the correct response is listed in the Answer Key. For short-answer items (such as fill-in-the-blank or matching), the correct letter, word, or phrase is listed.

In some cases where questions require the students to supply their own answers in phrases or sentences, the Answer Key provides the expected response or the factual information required. However, the content and wording of the students' answers may vary from what is listed in the Answer Key. In these cases the Answer Key should be used only as a guideline for determining whether students' responses are correct or not.

Scoring Tests: Content and Skills

To score the Content and Skills sections, use the Answer Key to mark each answer correct or incorrect. To determine a score for each section, add up the number of items answered correctly (for example, 3 of 5, 7 of 10, or 16 of 20).

To find a percentage score, divide the number answered correctly by the total number of items. Examples

$3 \div 5 = .60$, or 60%
$7 \div 10 = .70$, or 70%
$16 \div 20 = .80$, or 80%

Scoring Tests: Writing

To score the Writing section, use the Answer Key to evaluate each student's responses. The Answer Key describes the characteristics of an *Excellent* response and an *Adequate* response for each question. You may score the student's response as Excellent, Adequate, or Not Adequate based on the criteria listed in the Answer Key. Or, you may want to rate each of the student's responses on a 4-point scale, as explained on the next page.

Passing Scores

The Chapter Tests and Unit Tests are based on the content and skills taught in the chapter or the unit and are scored in relation to a criterion, or passing, score. In the Content and Skills sections, the recommended passing score is 70% (4 of 5, 7 of 10, or 14 of 20 items answered correctly). For the Writing section, students should achieve a score of at least *adequate* on each question, or at least 2 on the 4-point scale. (These are recommended passing scores; you may want to adjust them upward or downward for your students.)

Alternative Scoring Method for Writing: Using a 4-Point Scale

For the Writing section of each test, responses are intended to be scored as *Excellent, Adequate,* or *Not Adequate*. However, you may want to use an alternative method of scoring each student's responses on a scale of 1–4 (or 0 for an unscorable response). Each response may be awarded zero to four points depending on its accuracy and completeness. For example, students who provide a partial response to an exercise might receive one point, while students who give a full and outstanding response would receive four points. (A student who does not respond to a question or whose response is for some reason unscorable would receive zero points.)

To score students' responses on a 4-point scale, use the rating scale defined below. If you wish to convert scores on the 4-point scale to percentage scores, add the scores from both questions (for example, 2 + 3 = 5) and then use this conversion chart.

Conversion Chart	
Number of Points	**Percentage Score**
1	13%
2	25%
3	38%
4	50%
5	63%
6	75%
7	88%
8	100%

4-Point Rating Scale

4 Excellent. The student makes an outstanding response that includes all or most of the elements listed in the Answer Key. This score indicates that the student not only understands the necessary information and concepts but also exhibits additional insight into their meaning and importance.

3 Good. The student makes an above-average response that includes many of the elements listed in the Answer Key for both an adequate and an excellent response, indicating that the student has a firm grasp of the necessary concepts and information.

2 Fair. The student makes a satisfactory response that includes the elements listed in the Answer Key for an adequate response, indicating that the student has satisfactory knowledge and understanding of the necessary concepts and information.

1 Poor. The student makes a minimal response that does not include the elements listed in the Answer Key for an adequate response, indicating that the student has not learned or does not understand the necessary concepts and information.

0 No Response. The student did not respond to the exercise, or the response is illegible or for some other reason unscorable.

Scoring Performance Assessments
Each Performance Assessment includes a scoring rubric designed to help you evaluate each student's performance. The rubric describes the characteristics of the project on a 4-point scale: Excellent, Good, Fair, Poor (or Unscorable). Use the scoring rubric to score each student's work as a 4, 3, 2, 1, or 0. (In percentage scores, 4 = 100%, 3 = 75%, 2 = 50%, 1 = 25%.)

Portfolio Assessment Opportunities
The Performance Assessments are ideal activities for self-assessment, peer assessment, and inclusion in a portfolio. The "Portfolio Opportunity" guidelines suggest ways to engage students in evaluating their own work through self-assessment or peer assessment before displaying their work or placing it in their portfolios.

Self-Assessment and Peer Assessment
Students can learn a great deal from understanding and applying the standards of good work to their own achievements. In using the Performance Assessments, encourage students to assess their own work by pointing out what they think is good about it and what they think they might do better next time. You might want to have them complete the Self-Assessment Checklist on page T9 after they have completed a Think and Write activity or Unit Project (or other type of project activity).

When students have become familiar with self-assessment, have them practice peer assessment by working with partners. Encourage students to assess the work of others by pointing out positive aspects of it and discussing what they think is good about the other student's work. You may want to model this process for students so they understand the positive tone that should be applied. You might want to have them complete the Peer Assessment Checklist on page T10 to assess a student's work, a partner's work, or a group's work on a Think and Write activity, Unit Project, or other activity.

Group Assessment
In many projects and activities, students will be working with partners or in groups. To assess an individual's performance in a group situation, you can gather information through observation of the students as they work, through conferences with students in which they discuss their work, through self-assessments, and through peer assessments. You may want to use the Group Assessment Chart on page T11 to help evaluate and record individual performances.

Class Summary Chart
To develop a profile of student performance on the assessments for each unit, you may want to record the Unit Test and Unit Performance Assessment scores on the Class Summary Chart on page T12. From the student's test scores and Performance Assessment results, you can determine an overall rating of the student's performance for each unit. This overall rating may be expressed on the 4-point scale, as a percentage score, or as a letter grade.

Self-Assessment Checklist

Name _____ **Date** _____

Activity or Project _____

1. What did you do in this activity or project?
   _____
   _____

2. What parts of the activity or project did you do well?
   _____
   _____

3. What could you do better next time to improve your work?
   _____
   _____

4. What did you learn from this activity or project?
   _____
   _____

5. What did you like best about this activity or project?
   _____
   _____

Peer Assessment Checklist

Name _____ **Date** _____

Activity or Project _____

1. What did your classmate do in this activity or project?
   _____
   _____

2. If you worked with your classmate on this activity, tell what parts you did. (If you did not work with your classmate, skip to question 3.)
   _____
   _____

3. What was the best thing your classmate did?
   _____
   _____

4. How would you rate your classmate's work? (Circle one)

   Excellent	Good	Fair	Needs Improvement

5. What suggestions would you make to help your classmate do better next time?
   _____
   _____
   _____

Group Assessment Chart

Class _____ Activity or Project _____

Directions. Rate each individual's performance as 4, 3, 2, 1, or 0 on each of the criteria listed below.
(4 = Excellent, 3 = Good, 2 = Fair, 1 = Poor, 0 = Unscorable)

Student Names																
Criteria																
Participates in group work																
Contributes to project success																
Listens to others																
Asks and answers questions																
Stays on task																
Cooperates with others																
Offers positive suggestions																
Exhibits leadership																
Compliments and encourages others																
Overall Rating																

Regions • Using Assessment

CLASS SUMMARY CHART

Class _____ Unit _____

Student Name	Unit Test: Content and Skills	Unit Test: Writing	Performance Assessment	Overall Rating

Part 2

Answer Key

Contents

Answer Key T14–T26

Chapter 1

Content

1. c
2. a
3. b
4. c
5. b
6. Appalachian Mountains
7. rain and snow
8. St. Lawrence Seaway
9. recycling
10. climate

Skills

1. Denver, 5,000 ft.
2. Boston, 0 ft.
3. Lincoln, 1,000 ft.
4. Santa Fe, 7,000 ft.
5. Below Sea Level–700 ft.

Writing

1. An adequate response will make a logical inference about regional variations in climate and forest resources. For example, colder northern regions tend to have needleleaf forests. An excellent response will explain further, noting that in the warmer Southeast, mixed forests tend to grow, and so on.
2. An adequate response will suggest that this verse describes the Interior Plains and the Rocky Mountains. An excellent response will draw specific conclusions based on the chapter. For example, the "amber waves of grain" may be growing somewhere in the Interior Plains. The "spacious skies" might be in Oklahoma or Texas. The "purple mountain majesties" may be the Rockies or another mountain chain in the United States. The "fruited plain" may be part of the Interior Plains or even the Coastal Plains.

Chapter 2

Content

1. b
2. a
3. a
4. d
5. b
6. ancestor
7. region
8. Native Americans
9. enslaved Africans
10. economy

Skills

1. NO
2. YES
3. NO
4. YES
5. YES

Chapter 2, Continued

Writing

1. An adequate response will note that highways help link different parts of the country. Highways allow businesses to transport raw materials and finished goods. Highways allow Americans with different backgrounds to share their services, products, and traditions with one another. An excellent response will give specific examples of how highways help bring Americans together. For example, people from different regions can share their traditions by visiting one another. They can share products by transporting them from one region to another—Mexican food produced in the Southwest can be enjoyed in other regions.

2. An adequate response will note that all citizens have the right to use the highways, as well as the responsibility to help pay for the highways through taxes. Citizens can influence government decisions by contacting their representatives and sometimes by voting in referendums. An excellent response will give other examples of rights and responsibilities, such as the right to safe driving or protection from other drivers, and the responsibility to drive safely or to keep the highways clean.

Unit 1

Content and Skills

1. b
2. a
3. c
4. d
5. b
6. d
7. a
8. c
9. b
10. c
11. geography
12. basin
13. Rocky Mountains
14. elevation map
15. gravity
16. St. Lawrence Seaway
17. culture
18. democratic republic
19. Senate
20. free enterprise

Writing

1. An adequate response will clearly state where the student would live and give a reason related to climate. For example, "I would live in the Southwest because I like hot weather and I don't like snow." An excellent response will explain further by relating climate to personal goals. For example, "I would like to live somewhere where the seasons change because I enjoy all kinds of weather, and someday I would like to work in the shipping industry. For these reasons, I would choose the Northwest or the area near the Great Lakes."

2. An adequate response will state that Americans have different ethnic heritages, but similar rights and responsibilities. It will cite at least one example of each. An excellent response will cite several specific examples. For example, Americans of different ethnic backgrounds have differences in customs. Americans in different parts of the country have different jobs and skills. All United States citizens share certain rights (such as, the right to vote) and responsibilities (such as, the duty to pay taxes).

Chapter 3

Content

1. d
2. a
3. d
4. c
5. b
6. mouth
7. cash crop
8. coal
9. delta
10. wetlands

Skills

1. Much of Georgia is covered by pine forests.
2. Georgia produces more pecans and peanuts than any other state.
3. Georgia has a mild climate.
4. Georgia drivers creep along or skid on snowy roads.
5. Many of Georgia's rivers are dammed.
6. Lies on the Gulf of Mexico
7. Lies between Texas and Mississippi
8. What are Louisiana's natural resources?
9. Produces rice, sugarcane, and sweet potatoes
10. Produces shrimp, fish, and oysters from Gulf of Mexico

Writing

1. An adequate response will mention three special features of the Mississippi. An excellent response will mention four or more features, such as: The Mississippi has an enormous river basin; the Mississippi River basin drains land in a tremendous area of the country; the river often changes its course; goods from all over the country travel down the Mississippi; each day, the Mississippi carries tons of fine soil to its mouth, which is gradually being pushed farther and farther out into the Gulf of Mexico; many important cities have grown up along this river; its name in the Algonkian language is Misi Sipi ("big water" or "father of waters").

2. An adequate response will list five important resources in the Southeast (oil, coal, zinc, bauxite, and forests) and identify at least one state in which each resource is found. An excellent response will list all five resources and identify two or more states in which each resource is found. Forests are located in Florida, Georgia, Mississippi, Arkansas, Alabama, Virginia, Louisiana, and South Carolina. Bauxite is mined in Alabama, Louisiana, Arkansas, and Florida. Zinc is mined in Tennessee and Kentucky. There is oil in Louisiana, Alabama, Mississippi, and Kentucky, and there is coal in Tennessee, Alabama, Kentucky, North Carolina, Virginia, and West Virginia.

Chapter 4

Content

1. b
2. a
3. a
4. d
5. d
6. Trail of Tears
7. House of Burgesses
8. Declaration of Independence
9. civil rights movement
10. high technology

Skills

Events should be located correctly on the time line:

1789: North Carolina accepts U.S. Constitution
1795: University of North Carolina opens
1840: North Carolina's first public school opens
1868: North Carolina readmitted to the Union
1951: UNC at Chapel Hill admits first African American students

Writing

1. An adequate response will give two reasons to explain why the Cherokee removal was cruel; an excellent response will give three or more reasons. Examples: The Cherokee were forced off their land to make room for white settlers; their journey was hundreds of miles; they suffered from cold and disease; thousands of Cherokee died before they reached Oklahoma.
2. An adequate response will give one cause and one effect. An excellent response will give two or more causes and effects. Causes: In 1955 an African American woman named Rosa Parks was arrested in Montgomery, Alabama, for refusing to give up her seat on a bus as the law required. African Americans angry about Parks's arrest decided to boycott, or refuse to ride, Montgomery's buses. Effects: Many people joined the boycott. Dr. Martin Luther King, Jr., became famous for leading the boycott. Eventually, the city changed the law and allowed African Americans to sit anywhere they wanted on the city's buses.

Unit 2

Content and Skills

1. c
2. d
3. d
4. a
5. b
6. d
7. c
8. b
9. c
10. a
11. Sequoyah
12. Tahlequah
13. Thomas Jefferson
14. House of Burgesses
15. New Orleans
16. Frederick Douglass
17. Abraham Lincoln
18. Rosa Parks
19. Martin Luther King, Jr.
20. Gandhi

Unit 2, Continued

Writing

1. An adequate response will state that Florida has a longer growing season because it is warmer or has higher temperatures in the winter. An excellent response will explain other causes. For example, Florida is warmer because it is farther south and more of its land area is on the ocean. Virginia is cooler because it is farther north and has mountains, and higher elevation and greater latitude generally result in lower temperatures.

2. An adequate response will note that Tubman was a slave who escaped from slavery and served as a conductor on the Underground Railroad. An excellent response will include more details. (Example: Like most African Americans living in the United States at the time, Harriet Tubman was a slave. Like many slaves, Tubman was treated cruelly. As a child, she was beaten so badly by an overseer that she had blackouts the rest of her life. Tubman escaped from slavery and made her way north on the Underground Railroad. She decided to help other slaves to escape and risked her life and freedom many times by secretly returning to the South. When war broke out, Tubman served as a spy in the South.)

Chapter 5

Content

1. d
2. c
3. a
4. c
5. d
6. b
7. d
8. e
9. a
10. c

Skills

1. Charlotte, NC
2. 95°W
3. Santa Fe, NM
4. Memphis, TN
5. about 25°N, 80°W

Writing

1. An adequate response will indicate that fishing is probably important to the economy of Maine, since the state has a long shoreline. The response should indicate that fishing is probably less important to New Hampshire's economy since this state has a very short shoreline. An excellent response may mention Maine's jagged shoreline, which offers many safe places for fishing boats to dock, or may state that fishing might be important to only one small part of New Hampshire.

2. An adequate response will mention at least one aspect of climate (such as, temperature, precipitation, seasons) and geography (such as, mountains, plain, rivers, coastlines) and relate these to life in a given region. An excellent response will mention two or more aspects of climate and two or more aspects of geography. Example: The Middle West has large areas of flat land. It also has long summers with a large amount of rainfall. These conditions support farming, which is an important part of life in the Middle West.

Chapter 6

Content

1. a
2. d
3. d
4. a
5. b
6. Boston
7. Ellis Island
8. Onondaga
9. Argentina
10. Boswash

Skills

(Answers in 1-5 may vary.)

1. The Iroquois needed to join together to stop fighting among themselves.
2. Iroquois women were powerful, or women controlled the Confederacy.
3. The United States wanted immigrants to be able to work after they arrived.
4. Machines increased the speed of work and transportation.
5. Immigrants came to the United States to find jobs.
6. 1910
7. 1890
8. 1900–1910
9. 1870–1880
10. 1910 to 1920

Writing

1. An adequate response will indicate that most United States families live in suburban areas since the largest portion of the graph represents metropolitan areas outside cities, which are suburbs. An excellent response will indicate what portion of United States families live in each area. Example: According to the graph, about half of all families live in suburbs, about a quarter of all families live in rural areas outside metropolitan areas, and another quarter live in cities.
2. An adequate response will mention two of the following factors; an excellent response will mention three or more. Factors: Many ships carrying immigrants to the United States landed in New York City; factory jobs were plentiful in New York City during the huge wave of immigration to the United States at the turn of the century; many immigrants who settled in New York City may have been joining family members and/or neighbors who had previously immigrated; many immigrants were poor and unable to establish their own businesses in the New York City area or elsewhere.

UNIT 3

Content and Skills

1. b
2. d
3. a
4. c
5. d
6. a
7. c
8. b
9. b
10. d
11. bays and harbors
12. broadleaf and needleleaf trees
13. rivers
14. Appalachian Mountains
15. seasons
16. circle graph
17. global grid
18. longitude
19. line graph
20. latitude

Writing

1. An adequate response will mention two or more areas which the map indicates are chiefly forest land (for example, New England, central Pennsylvania) and explain that the large expanses of forests in these areas would have the most impressive displays of autumn leaves. An excellent response may also mention that manufacturing centers and areas of cropland would be less impressive since these areas have fewer trees.
2. An adequate response will identify the type of community correctly, indicate whether the community is likely to grow, and offer a logical basis for this opinion. An excellent response will include more detail and more than one logical reason for growth. Example: My community is a suburb outside a major city. It will probably grow a lot in the future because several companies have moved here and people who work for the companies will probably live in our community.

CHAPTER 7

Content

1. b
2. c
3. a
4. c
5. d
6. C
7. B
8. A
9. A
10. B

Skills

1. Map B
2. Map A
3. Map A
4. about 8 miles
5. about 8 miles

Chapter 7, Continued

Writing

1. An adequate response will mention that the region has fertile soil, but it also has short growing seasons and occasional drought. An excellent response will explain in more depth that the region's soil and climate provide ideal conditions for raising corn (on the Central Plains) and wheat (on the Great Plains), but the hot summers, cold winters, occasional drought, short growing season, and severe storms including tornadoes can make farming difficult. Students may also refer to the "lake effect," which provides a gentler climate and better farming near the Great Lakes.

2. An adequate response will note that steel production increased greatly between 1891 and 1910 because of the growth of industry in the United States but production fell recently in the late 1980s because cheaper steel was available from Japan and Europe. An excellent response will explain that the growth in steel production from 1891 to 1910 was due to developments in United States manufacturing, such as the spread of the railroads, the growth of the automobile industry, and the building of skyscrapers. In recent years, foreign steel was cheaper because their factories were newer and used modern technology. United States steel mills became more competitive in the 1990s with the use of new technology.

Chapter 8

Content

1. b
2. d
3. c
4. a
5. d
6. George Custer
7. John Deere
8. Jean Baptiste Point du Sable
9. Abraham Lincoln
10. Henry Ford

Skills

1. team/territory
2. textbook/thaw
3. Vol. 17
4. Vol. 12
5. Vol. 4

Writing

1. An adequate response will state that white settlers became interested in the Black Hills when gold was discovered there, and the conflict over the region resulted in war. An excellent response will explain the events in more depth. For example, the Black Hills had been promised forever to the Lakota by the United States government. When gold was discovered, white settlers invaded the Lakota territory, violating the Treaty of 1868. Instead of upholding the treaty, the government sent soldiers to put down the Lakota disturbance. War resulted, and the Lakota eventually had to surrender.

2. An adequate response will indicate that today there are fewer family farms and more competition with agribusiness, and that farmers rely more on technology than they used to. Yet the Middle West is still the "breadbasket" for the United States. An excellent response will also mention specific technological developments, such as the use of computers to keep track of crops and better seed to improve harvests. It may also mention that many of today's farmers work directly with food-processing companies. Unpredictable weather and protecting the soil are things that haven't changed.

UNIT 4

Content and Skills

1. b
2. d
3. a
4. b
5. d
6. d
7. a
8. c
9. c
10. a
11. drought
12. mall
13. map scale
14. scale strip
15. steel plow
16. buffalo
17. mass production
18. guide words
19. CD-ROM
20. combine

Writing

1. An adequate response will mention that in most of the Interior Plains, summers are hot and winters are very cold. Corn is the major crop grown in the Central Plains, while wheat is the major crop grown in the Great Plains. An excellent response will extend the comparison to include other information. For example, the Central Plains have lower elevations and are more humid than the Great Plains.

2. An adequate response will point out that the farm population has dropped steadily in Nebraska since the early part of the century. This change reflects the fact that thousands of family farms in the Middle West have gone out of business in recent years. An excellent response will explain that farmers must compete with agribusiness, and a big company isn't as easily harmed by a bad season as a small farmer is. Also, many young people today move to the cities, part of a national trend.

CHAPTER 9

Content

1. c
2. a
3. d
4. d
5. c
6. Grand Canyon
7. Sonoran Desert
8. Texas
9. Houston
10. Tulsa

Skills

1–3. Any three of the following sentences:

The Grand Canyon is the most spectacular sight in the world. They should visit the north rim instead. The view from the north rim is very exciting. All of the tourist attractions ruin the experience of visiting the canyon. You will appreciate it most if you go to a quiet spot on the north rim and just admire the view.

4–5. Any two of the following sentences:

More than four million people visit it each year. Most tourists visit the south rim of the canyon. The north rim is 1,200 feet higher than the south rim. The south rim has many restaurants and viewing spots complete with telescopes.

CHAPTER 9, CONTINUED

Writing

1. An adequate response will state that people in other parts of the United States depend on the economy of the Southwest because they use products from that part of the country. Some examples should be included, such as oil and cotton from Texas, oil from Oklahoma, electrical devices from Arizona. An excellent response will identify products in everyday life that come from the industries shown on the map (examples: pens from petrochemicals, clothes from cotton, hamburgers from ranching).

2. An adequate response will give at least one advantage and one disadvantage of the Southwest. For example, it has a dry climate, sunny weather, oil, and tourism; but it is very hot and has little water. An excellent response will list two or more advantages and disadvantages, and it may describe less obvious features. For example, the Southwest has beautiful scenery, and most of the region experiences little change in the seasons.

CHAPTER 10

Content

1. b
2. d
3. a
4. b
5. c
6. Window Rock
7. Santa Fe
8. Dinetah
9. Sun Belt
10. Kitt Peak

Skills

1. primary source
2. secondary source
3. The writer of the first source uses words such as *I* and *my* when describing cowboy life.
4. The writer of the second source talks about cowboys as other people and discusses what they used to do rather than what they are doing in the present.
5. The first source gives a better understanding because a cowboy is telling of his own experiences and feelings.

Writing

1. An adequate response will point out that the Southwest has more hot weather than most other parts of the country. As a result, few people lived there in the past, although the population of the Southwest later increased with the development of air conditioning and cars. An excellent response will explain other reasons for these changes. For example, new industries and a dry, sunny climate have actually attracted more people to move there.

2. An adequate response will give at least two examples of traditions carried on today. Examples: herding sheep and other animals, doing traditional crafts such as weaving, speaking Navajo, and living in hogans. An excellent response will suggest that carrying on traditions is important for preserving the Navajo culture.

Unit 5

Content and Skills

1. b
2. a
3. c
4. d
5. d
6. c
7. a
8. b
9. b
10. d
11. butte
12. dry farming
13. drought
14. aquifer
15. petroleum
16. refinery
17. hogan
18. mission
19. feedlot
20. vaquero

Writing

1. An adequate response will explain how one major environmental characteristic has affected Southwesterners, such as low rainfall causing the Dust Bowl and leading farmers to use special dry farming techniques. An excellent response will analyze the results of several conditions, such as hot weather keeping the population low in the past and the presence of petroleum deposits leading to major industrial development.

2. An adequate response will explain that in the 1600s and 1700s the Southwest was a colony of Spain with Santa Fe as its capital. Eventually the Spanish built missions throughout the region. The purpose of the missions was to convert the Native Americans to Christianity. Colonists also began huge farms called ranchos to raise cattle. An excellent response will describe the missions in greater detail and will also mention that Spanish culture still remains in the language, customs, and buildings of the Southwest.

Chapter 11

Content

1. a
2. d
3. b
4. c
5. d
6. e
7. d
8. a
9. c
10. b

Skills

1. Arrow should point to the interstate highway (5) running north and south.
2. a local road (A16)
3. a local road (A16)
4. route 299
5. a state highway

Chapter 11, Continued

Writing

1. An adequate response will state at least three different products made from wood, such as paper, houses, furniture, rayon, turpentine, rubber. It will also give at least one reason for careful use, such as: if forests vanish, many types of wildlife will die; if we use up our forests, we will be unable to make many important products, and many people will lose their jobs; deforestation threatens the quality of our air, since forests produce oxygen. An excellent response will draw connections between products that we use and the need to use resources carefully.

2. An adequate response will state at least two physical extremes. Examples: The West has the northernmost part of our country (Alaska) and the southernmost part (Hawaii); it has the wettest place in the country (in Hawaii) and the driest (Death Valley, California); it has high mountains and deserts. An excellent response will list more than two physical extremes or discuss other less obvious extremes. For example, the West has an enormous diversity of population (Polynesians and Asian Americans in Hawaii, Inuit in Alaska, Hispanic and many others in California, and so on); it is more spread out than any other region, since it includes Alaska and Hawaii.

Chapter 12

Content

1. c
2. d
3. c
4. a
5. d
6. d
7. a
8. b
9. e
10. c

Skills

1. Many people moved to the West because of problems back home.
2. People living in the West have come from many countries.
3. Many people moved to the West to find jobs (or to make money).
4. Many people living in the West have come from Asia.
5. People from all over the world have immigrated to the West to find new opportunities.

Writing

1. An adequate response will state that this belief led to a demand that women get the vote. It should also mention at least two of the following events: Wyoming was the first state where women got the right to vote, and other Western territories and states followed soon thereafter; the first woman judge was appointed in Wyoming; the first woman elected to the House of Representatives was from Montana; the first woman governor was elected in Wyoming. An excellent response will discuss the efforts of Susan B. Anthony and Elizabeth Cady Stanton as they toured the West speaking out for women's rights, will detail the "firsts" achieved in Western states, and might explore why such progress was achieved (such as, the pioneers in the West seemed to be more open to new ideas).

CHAPTER 12, CONTINUED

2. An adequate response will state what each group did: the Polynesians brought new plants and livestock; the European and American traders cut down trees and set up pineapple and sugarcane plantations; the immigrants came to work on the plantations; American business leaders overthrew the queen. An excellent response will demonstrate a deeper understanding of the effects of these changes. For example, the Polynesians changed the environment of Hawaii by importing coconuts, taro, pigs, and dogs; traders changed the environment and the economy by exploiting natural resources and building enormous plantations; immigrants changed the population and culture of the islands as they soon outnumbered native inhabitants; business leaders made permanent changes in the islands by making it a part of the United States.

UNIT 6

Content and Skills

1. b
2. d
3. b
4. c
5. a
6. b
7. d
8. c
9. a
10. d
11. Coast Ranges
12. Central Valley Project
13. Polynesia
14. Queen Liliuokalani
15. California Gold Rush
16. ghost town
17. transcontinental railroad
18. Thomas Edison
19. Brazil
20. Chico Mendes

Writing

1. An adequate response will state that the tables show that Americans are using more lumber every year but less lumber is being produced in the West in recent years. The decrease in production of lumber will hurt the economy of the West because the lumber industry will make less money, produce fewer goods, and have fewer jobs. An excellent response will explain that the United States is using more lumber from other places than the West to build homes, schools, and other important buildings. However, if we do not continue to conserve Western lumber, the resources of the West will be used up eventually, and its economy and environment will suffer even more.

2. An adequate response will state that Americans buy many products from Japan (such as cars, sound systems, VCRs) and Japan buys products from the United States (such as movies, music, timber, petroleum). An excellent response will demonstrate a deeper understanding of how the two countries are interdependent economically and culturally. For example, it might note that Japan has fewer raw materials than the United States and, therefore, must create and export finished products. The United States buys these well-made products but exports to Japan its raw materials (timber, oil) and parts of its culture (music, movies).

Part 3

Chapter and Unit Tests

Name: _____ Date: _____

CONTENT

Fill in the circle before the correct answer.

1. Which landform is a high, flat area that rises steeply above the land around it?
   - (a) mountain
   - (b) basin
   - (c) plateau
   - (d) coastal plain

2. The Interior Plains area of the United States is known for its _____.
   - (a) rich soil
   - (b) extremely low rainfall
   - (c) tall mountains
   - (d) ocean breezes

3. An area will most likely have cold winters if it _____.
   - (a) is close to the ocean
   - (b) is far from the equator
   - (c) has a low elevation
   - (d) has little precipitation

4. Which is a renewable source of energy?
   - (a) oil
   - (b) coal
   - (c) solar power
   - (d) natural gas

5. What happens to soil if it is farmed over and over?
   - (a) It gets richer.
   - (b) It gets worn out.
   - (c) It gets polluted.
   - (d) It produces energy.

Write an answer from the box to complete each sentence.

| St. Lawrence Seaway | rain and snow | recycling |
| Appalachian Mountains | climate | |

6. The _____ stretch all the way from Maine to Alabama.

7. _____ are two forms of precipitation.

8. The _____ allows ships from both Canada and the United States to travel from the Great Lakes to the Atlantic Ocean.

9. _____ is the process of making used products into new products.

10. The pattern of weather in a place over a long period of time is called its _____.

Name: Date:

SKILLS

Use the map below to answer each question.

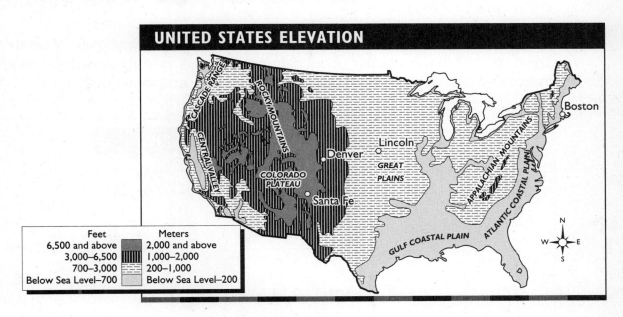

Draw a line from each city to its approximate height above sea level.

1. Denver   7,000 feet above sea level

2. Boston   5,000 feet above sea level

3. Lincoln   1,000 feet above sea level

4. Santa Fe   0 feet above sea level

5. What is the elevation of the Atlantic Coastal Plain?
   _____

Name: _____ Date: _____

WRITING

Write a short paragraph to answer each question. If you need more room, continue writing on the back of this page.

1. Look at the map showing forest resources in North America. Now think of what you have learned in the chapter about different climates in North America. Using the map, what can you tell about our country's climate and forest resources?

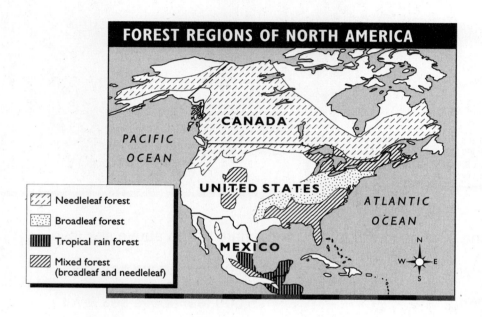

_____
_____
_____

2. Read the beginning of "America, the Beautiful" by Katherine Lee Bates.
   O beautiful for spacious skies,
   For amber waves of grain,
   For purple mountain majesties
   Above the fruited plain!

   Which parts of our country do you think the lines in the poem refer to? Support your opinions with facts you learned in this chapter.

_____
_____
_____

Regions   3   Chapter 1

Name: _____   Date: _____

CONTENT

Fill in the circle before the correct answer.

1. An ethnic group is made up of people who _____.
   - (a) share the same opinion
   - (b) share the same heritage
   - (c) live in the same neighborhood
   - (d) recently moved to the United States

2. In which part of the economy do most Americans work?
   - (a) services
   - (b) farming
   - (c) industry
   - (d) manufacturing

3. The job of the United States Congress is to _____.
   - (a) make laws
   - (b) lead the military
   - (c) make sure laws are carried out
   - (d) deal with people who have broken the law

4. Which of these is one of the five regions of the United States?
   - (a) Interior Plains
   - (b) Rocky Mountains
   - (c) Mississippi River valley
   - (d) Southwest

5. One responsibility of the President of the United States is to _____.
   - (a) make laws
   - (b) lead the military
   - (c) make money
   - (d) improve our schools

Write a word or phrase from the box to answer each question.

| Native Americans | economy | enslaved Africans |
| region | ancestor | |

6. What is the term for a person born before other generations of the same family? _____

7. What is the name for an area with common features that make it different from other areas? _____

8. Who were the first people to live in North America? _____

9. Which group of people were forced to come to America against their will? _____

10. What term describes the way a country uses resources to meet people's needs and wants? _____

Regions   1   Chapter 2

Name: _____ Date: _____

SKILLS

Read the information in the box. Then answer the questions below.

> In one community there is a "leash law" for dogs. It says that dog owners must keep dogs on their own property or keep them on a leash. The community will soon hold a referendum on whether or not to apply the leash law to pet cats. If the law is passed, then cat owners will have to either keep their pets inside, make their cats stay within their own property, or use a leash when their cats are on public sidewalks. Do you think you would vote for this referendum? How would you decide? Study the arguments in favor of the law and against it.

In Favor

- Cats will kill fewer birds.
- Cats will not dig up neighbors' yards.
- Cats won't disturb neighbors by making noise at night.
- Indoor cats get fewer diseases and fleas.

Against

- Cats dislike leashes more than dogs do.
- Cats will get less exercise.
- Walls and fences seldom keep cats in a yard.
- Cats will kill fewer pests, such as mice.

Next to each goal below, write YES if it would make you vote for the referendum and NO if it would make you vote against it.

1. Your goal is to get rid of mice and moles in your yard. _____

2. Your goal is to protect the birds that come to your feeder. _____

3. Your goal is to let your cat climb trees. _____

4. Your goal is to keep your cat from getting fleas. _____

5. Your goal is to protect your flower garden. _____

Name: _____ Date: _____

WRITING

Write a short paragraph to answer each question. If you need more room, continue writing on the back of this page.

1. What important role do highways play in the United States? Tell why highways are important to businesses and how they help Americans be more interdependent with one another.

   _____
   _____
   _____
   _____

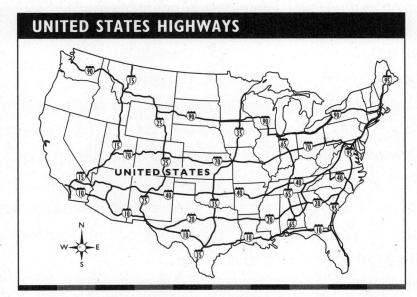

2. Think about the highways shown on the map. What rights and responsibilities do individual citizens have in connection with our nation's highways? How might citizens influence government decisions about where and when to build highways?

   _____
   _____
   _____
   _____

Name: _____ Date: _____

CONTENT AND SKILLS

Fill in the circle before the correct answer.

1. Which of these is a renewable resource?
   - (a) coal
   - (b) forests
   - (c) oil
   - (d) iron

2. A citizen of the United States has to be at least 18 years old to _____.
   - (a) vote in elections
   - (b) get a job
   - (c) finish school
   - (d) drive a car

3. What is the name of the plan written by the founders of the United States to describe our government and our most important laws?
   - (a) Declaration of Independence
   - (b) referendum
   - (c) Constitution
   - (d) democracy

4. Which branch of the United States government makes laws for the whole country?
   - (a) Supreme Court
   - (b) executive branch
   - (c) President
   - (d) Congress

5. What is it called when citizens vote for or against a proposed idea?
   - (a) decision
   - (b) referendum
   - (c) election
   - (d) free enterprise

6. Which of these resources cannot be replaced once it is used up?
   - (a) wood
   - (b) water
   - (c) soil
   - (d) oil

7. Which of these workers offers a service rather than makes a product?
   - (a) dentist
   - (b) baker
   - (c) farmer
   - (d) factory worker

8. Land far from the ocean tends to stay _____.
   - (a) mild all year long
   - (b) warmer in the winter
   - (c) hotter in the summer
   - (d) cooler in the summer

9. Which landform is shared by Canada and the United States?
   - (a) Great Basin
   - (b) Interior Plains
   - (c) Blue Ridge Mountains
   - (d) Coastal Plain

10. Which of these is a factor that affects climate?
    - (a) distance from highways
    - (b) time of day
    - (c) distance from the equator
    - (d) type of economy

Regions   Unit 1

Name: _____ Date: _____

CONTENT AND SKILLS

Write a word or phrase from the box to answer each question.

elevation map	Rocky Mountains	free enterprise
basin	geography	St. Lawrence Seaway
gravity	culture	democratic republic
Senate		

11. What is the name for the study of Earth and the things on it? _____

12. Which landform is a low, round area surrounded by higher land? _____

13. Which mountains stretch all through the western United States? _____

14. What kind of map shows the height of land above sea level? _____

15. What causes the water in a river to flow in a certain direction? _____

16. What project did the United States and Canada complete in 1959? _____

17. What is the name for the way of life that includes a people's language, beliefs, and customs? _____

18. What is the name for a government in which people pick representatives to run their country? _____

19. Which part of Congress has only two members from each state? _____

20. What is the name of a system in which people make their own business decisions? _____

Regions — Unit 1

Name: Date:

WRITING

Write a short paragraph to answer each question. If you need more room, continue writing on the back of this page.

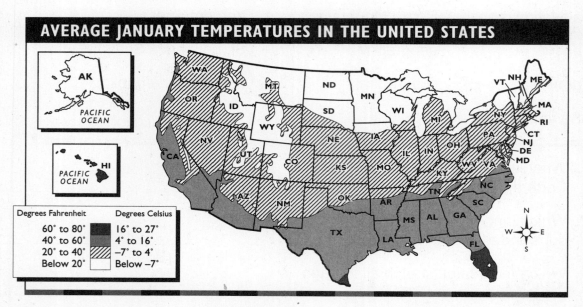

1. Suppose that you are an adult and you are going to choose the part of the United States where you will live. Look at the information on the map. Where will you decide to live and why?

   _____
   _____
   _____
   _____

2. Tell how Americans are different from one another and how they are similar. Think about their different ethnic backgrounds, customs, beliefs, and skills. Think about their rights and responsibilities.

   _____
   _____
   _____
   _____
   _____
   _____
   _____

Name: _____   Date: _____

CONTENT

Fill in the circle before the correct answer.

1. Which crop needs the longest growing season?
   - ⓐ corn
   - ⓑ wheat
   - ⓒ potatoes
   - ⓓ oranges

2. Many tourists are drawn to the Southeast by its _____.
   - ⓐ warm climate
   - ⓒ large cities
   - ⓑ clean water
   - ⓓ high mountains

3. The Aswan High Dam helps the people of Egypt by _____.
   - ⓐ emptying Lake Victoria
   - ⓒ protecting people from enemies
   - ⓑ controlling river transportation
   - ⓓ producing hydroelectric power

4. How is mining today different from mining 100 years ago?
   - ⓐ It is slower today.
   - ⓒ Technology has improved.
   - ⓑ It is more dangerous today.
   - ⓓ Miners use picks and shovels more often.

5. One of the most common dangers of working in a coal mine is _____.
   - ⓐ flooding
   - ⓑ a cave-in
   - ⓒ earthquakes
   - ⓓ shock

Write a word or phrase from the box to answer each question.

| mouth | cash crop | coal | delta | wetlands |

6. Which part of a river empties into a large body of water? _____

7. What is a crop that is grown to be sold? _____

8. Which mineral is valuable because it can be burned for heat? _____

9. What is formed when a river deposits soil at the place where it runs into the sea? _____

10. What helps control floods by soaking up water? _____

Regions   Chapter 3

Name: _____   Date: _____

SKILLS

Use the information in the paragraphs below to complete the cause-and-effect chart.

Georgia has seventeen major rivers. Many of these rivers were dammed during the 1930s. Damming the rivers created hydroelectric power and helped control flooding.

Georgia has fertile soil. It produces more peanuts and pecans than any other state. Pine forests cover much of the state. Georgia is a major producer of tar and turpentine—products made from its pine trees.

Georgia also has a mild climate. Georgians seldom see more than an inch of snow a year. When really cold weather does strike, Georgians may have a hard time! Since they aren't used to icy conditions, Georgia's drivers creep along or skid over snowy roads. Luckily, the bad weather seldom lasts long.

CAUSE	EFFECT
1.	1. Georgia is a major producer of tar and turpentine.
2. Georgia has fertile soil.	2.
3.	3. Georgians seldom see snow.
4. Georgians are not used to driving in icy conditions.	4.
5.	5. There is hydroelectric power in Georgia.

Name: _____ Date: _____

SKILLS

Read the paragraphs below. Use the information to complete the outline by filling in the blanks.

Louisiana

Louisiana is on the coast of the Gulf of Mexico. It lies between Texas to the west and Mississippi to the east. Its largest city is New Orleans, located near the mouth of the Mississippi River.

Louisiana has many natural resources. Half of the state's land area is covered by forests, which produce timber and pulp. The state's warm climate and rich soil make Louisiana a major producer of agricultural products. It is one of the country's leading producers of rice, sugarcane, and sweet potatoes. From the Gulf of Mexico, Louisiana produces shrimp, fish, and oysters. It also has great mineral wealth. Louisiana leads the country in the production of salt and sulfur. It ranks second in the production of oil and natural gas, much of which comes from offshore wells in the Gulf of Mexico.

Louisiana

I. Where is Louisiana?

6.   A. _____

7.   B. _____

8. II. _____

    A. Produces timber and pulp from its forests

9.   B. _____

10. C. _____

    D. Ranks second in production of oil and natural gas

Regions — Chapter 3

Name: _____ Date: _____

WRITING

Write a short paragraph to answer the following. If you need more room, continue writing on the back of this page.

1. The Mississippi River is unusual and important in many ways. Write a paragraph telling how this river is special.

   _____
   _____
   _____
   _____

2. What are some of the important natural resources in the Southeast? Where in the region are these resources located?

   _____
   _____
   _____
   _____

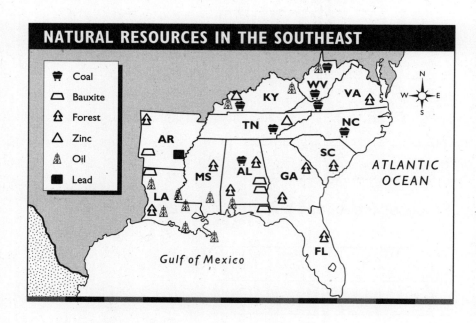

NATURAL RESOURCES IN THE SOUTHEAST

Regions   4   Chapter 3

Name: _____   Date: _____

CONTENT

Fill in the circle before the correct answer.

1. A Cherokee village was governed by _____.
   - ⓐ a single village chief
   - ⓑ a council of men
   - ⓒ the mothers of the village
   - ⓓ a group of men and women

2. Each symbol in Sequoyah's Cherokee alphabet represented a _____.
   - ⓐ syllable
   - ⓑ word
   - ⓒ letter
   - ⓓ thought

3. Who argued in 1774 that the British Parliament had no right to control Virginia's House of Burgesses?
   - ⓐ Thomas Jefferson
   - ⓑ the Royal Governor
   - ⓒ Jefferson Davis
   - ⓓ Frederick Douglass

4. India struggled to win its independence from _____.
   - ⓐ Canada
   - ⓑ South Africa
   - ⓒ China
   - ⓓ Great Britain

5. Eleven Southern states left the Union as a result of the _____.
   - ⓐ Emancipation Proclamation
   - ⓑ Underground Railroad
   - ⓒ destruction of many Southern cities
   - ⓓ election of Abraham Lincoln

Write a term from the box to complete each sentence.

| civil rights movement | high technology | Declaration of Independence |
| Trail of Tears | House of Burgesses | |

6. The Cherokee called their journey from the Southeast to Arkansas and Oklahoma the _____.

7. In colonial Virginia, only white men who owned property were allowed to vote in elections for the _____.

8. Thomas Jefferson wrote the _____ to explain why the 13 American colonies should no longer be ruled by England.

9. Martin Luther King, Jr., was a leader of the _____.

10. Industries that use computers and other electronics to meet new needs are said to use _____.

Name: _____   Date: _____

SKILLS

Study the time line. Then look at the list of other events from North Carolina's history. Complete the time line by writing the additional events below the time line in the correct places.

Events in North Carolina History

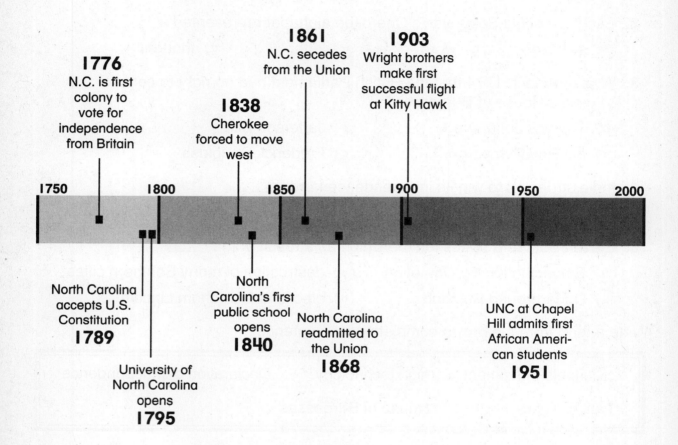

Events

1. In 1868 North Carolina was readmitted to the Union.

2. In 1951 the University of North Carolina at Chapel Hill admitted its first African American students.

3. The University of North Carolina opened in 1795.

4. North Carolina's first public school opened in 1840.

5. In 1789 North Carolina accepted the United States Constitution.

Regions   Chapter 4

Name: _____ Date: _____

WRITING

Write a short paragraph to answer each question. If you need more room, continue writing on the back of this page.

1. A Georgia soldier who helped oversee the forced move of the Cherokee from the Southeast later described his experience:

   I fought through the War Between the States *[Civil War],* and have seen men shot to pieces by the thousands, but the Cherokee Removal was the cruelest work I ever knew.

   Source: *The Cherokee Removal* by Glen Fleischmann, Watts, N.Y., 1971

   Why do you think he described the removal as "cruel"? Use what you have learned about why the Cherokee left and what happened to them on their journey to answer this question.

   _____
   _____
   _____
   _____
   _____

2. What were the causes and effects of the Montgomery bus boycott? Describe the events that led up to the boycott. Name the leader who became famous as a result. Make sure you describe the events in the order in which they happened.

   _____
   _____
   _____
   _____
   _____

Regions — Chapter 4

Name: _____ Date: _____

CONTENT AND SKILLS

Fill in the circle before the correct answer.

1. A place where ships load and unload goods is called a _____.
   - (a) basin
   - (b) delta
   - (c) port
   - (d) source

2. The number of days in a year when it is warm enough for crops to grow is known as a _____.
   - (a) wetland
   - (b) harvest
   - (c) cash crop
   - (d) growing season

3. Why does the Mississippi River change course less now than it used to?
   - (a) The area has less precipitation now than it used to have.
   - (b) The river is not as deep as it used to be.
   - (c) There are more people living along the banks of the river now.
   - (d) Engineers have built walls along parts of the river.

4. The Mississippi is fed by many smaller rivers called _____.
   - (a) tributaries
   - (b) deltas
   - (c) mouths
   - (d) basins

5. Peanuts grow well in the Southeast because the region has _____.
   - (a) little rain
   - (b) a long growing season
   - (c) cold winters
   - (d) cool, wet summers

6. Which factor contributes to good crops in the Southeast?
   - (a) dry weather all year
   - (b) rivers
   - (c) coal deposits
   - (d) enough rain

7. Why were the Cherokee forced to move west in 1838?
   - (a) They could not grow crops.
   - (b) They could no longer hunt.
   - (c) White settlers wanted their land.
   - (d) Other Native Americans took their towns.

8. A Cherokee village was governed by _____.
   - (a) a group of women
   - (b) a council of men
   - (c) a single leader
   - (d) an elected president

9. Coal became a much more important fuel in the 1830s as a result of the development of _____.
   - (a) telephones
   - (b) wagons
   - (c) railroads
   - (d) cannons

10. Who helped improve conditions for coal miners?
    - (a) the miners' union
    - (b) the Confederacy
    - (c) Ulysses S. Grant
    - (d) Jefferson Davis

Name: _____   Date: _____

CONTENT AND SKILLS

Write the name from the box that best fits each description.

House of Burgesses	Thomas Jefferson
Martin Luther King, Jr.	Gandhi
Rosa Parks	Abraham Lincoln
Sequoyah	New Orleans
Frederick Douglass	Tahlequah

11. He invented a system of writing for the Cherokee language. _____

12. After the Trail of Tears, the Cherokee founded a new capital in this town in Oklahoma. _____

13. He wrote the Declaration of Independence. _____

14. This was a group of citizens who made laws for the colony of Virginia. _____

15. This city is near the mouth of the Mississippi River. _____

16. He was one of the best-known speakers and writers against slavery. _____

17. In the Emancipation Proclamation he declared that all slaves in the South were free. _____

18. The Montgomery bus boycott began when she refused to give up her seat on the bus to a white man. _____

19. This civil rights leader led the 1963 March on Washington and gave a famous speech that included the words "I have a dream." _____

20. He used nonviolent protest to help bring about change in India. _____

Name: _____ Date: _____

WRITING

Write a short paragraph to answer each question. If you need more room, continue writing on the back of this page.

1. Look at the chart showing average winter temperatures in different parts of Florida and Virginia. Florida has a longer growing season than Virginia. What is the cause of this difference?

State	Average Winter Temperatures
Florida	Northern Part — 54°F
	Southern Part — 67°F
Virginia	Mountains — 32°F
	Coast — 41°F

_____
_____
_____
_____
_____
_____

2. What does the story of Harriet Tubman show about the problems and struggles of African Americans during slavery? Write a paragraph describing her life.

_____
_____
_____
_____
_____
_____
_____

Name: _____   Date: _____

CONTENT

Fill in the circle before the correct answer.

1. Which is the largest group of mountains in the Northeast?
   - (a) Allegheny Mountains
   - (b) Catskill Mountains
   - (c) Green Mountains
   - (d) Appalachian Mountains

2. Forests cover much of the Northeast because this region has _____.
   - (a) only small amounts of pollution
   - (b) many hills and plateaus
   - (c) plenty of precipitation all year
   - (d) warm autumns and springs

3. The Northeast's first factories were powered by _____.
   - (a) rivers
   - (b) the sun
   - (c) gasoline
   - (d) the wind

4. Aquaculture is the business of raising fish in _____.
   - (a) bays or harbors
   - (b) rivers
   - (c) tanks or ponds
   - (d) the open sea

5. The most important part of the Swiss economy is _____.
   - (a) mining
   - (b) farming
   - (c) fishing
   - (d) manufacturing

Write the letter of each term next to the phrase that describes it.

a. timberline	c. canton	e. glacier
b. harbor	d. fall line	

6. _____ a place where boats can dock

7. _____ where mountains and plateaus meet a plain

8. _____ a huge sheet of ice that moves slowly across land

9. _____ the point at which it is too cold for trees to grow

10. _____ a state in the country of Switzerland

Name: _____   Date: _____

SKILLS

Use the map to answer the questions. Write your answers on the lines.

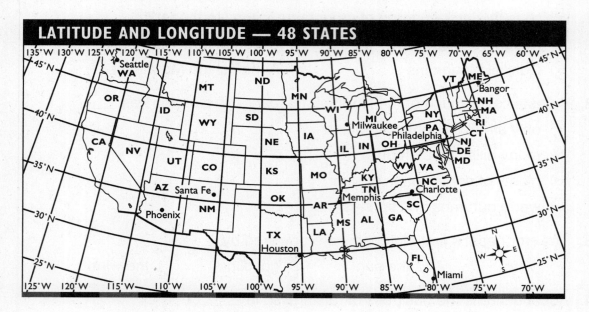

1. Which city is located at about 35°N, 80°W? _____

2. Which line of longitude passes through Houston, Texas? _____

3. Which city is located at about 36°N, 106°W? _____

4. Which city is located at about 35°N, 90°W? _____

5. What is the location of Miami, Florida? _____

Name: _____ Date: _____

WRITING

Write a short paragraph to answer each question. If you need more room, continue writing on the back of this page.

1. Look at the map. Do you think fishing is important to the economy of Maine? Do you think it is important to the economy of New Hampshire? Explain your answers.

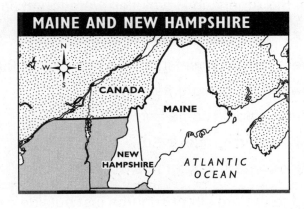

_____
_____
_____
_____
_____

2. Describe the climate and geography of your region. Explain how they are important to the people who live there.

_____
_____
_____
_____
_____
_____
_____

Regions 3 Chapter 5

| Name: | Date: |

CONTENT

Fill in the circle before the correct answer.

1. The main purpose of the Iroquois Confederacy was to _____.
   - (a) keep peace
   - (b) start new villages
   - (c) teach young Iroquois
   - (d) conquer the Mohawks

2. The first battles of the American Revolution were fought in _____.
   - (a) New York
   - (b) Pennsylvania
   - (c) Virginia
   - (d) Massachusetts

3. Which of these were called "sweatshops" in the early 1900s?
   - (a) businesses owned by immigrants
   - (b) countries that immigrants came from
   - (c) apartments where immigrants lived
   - (d) crowded factories where immigrants worked

4. Which of these led to the growth of suburbs just outside cities?
   - (a) new forms of transportation
   - (b) the need for more farms
   - (c) poor conditions in factories
   - (d) a decline in immigration

5. Buenos Aires has been influenced most by immigrants from _____.
   - (a) Asia
   - (b) Europe
   - (c) Africa
   - (d) North America

Complete each sentence with one of the places listed in the box below.

Onondaga   Boswash   Ellis Island   Boston   Argentina

6. Patriots first clashed with British soldiers in _____.

7. Immigrants stopped at _____ on their way to New York City.

8. Leaders of the Iroquois Confederacy met at _____.

9. Buenos Aires is the most important city in _____.

10. _____ is the name given to the Northeast's megalopolis.

Name: _____   Date: _____

SKILLS

Read the statements. Make your own conclusion from the statements and write it on the lines.

1. Iroquois groups fought over land and resources. Deganawida thought the Iroquois should join together. Hiawatha also urged the Iroquois to make peace and band together.

   _____
   _____

2. In the Iroquois Confederacy sachems were chosen by women from each group. Women could remove a sachem if they did not like his decisions.

   _____
   _____

3. When immigrants arrived at Ellis Island, doctors examined them to make sure they were healthy enough to work. Immigration officers asked them what kind of work they could do. They also asked the immigrants if they could read and write.

   _____
   _____

4. Garment workers could make clothes faster with a sewing machine than by hand. Goods were moved faster by railroads than by horse-drawn wagons.

   _____
   _____

5. Domingo came to the United States to find a job. Maria came to the United States because there were no job opportunities at home.

   _____
   _____

Name: _____ Date: _____

SKILLS

Use the graph to answer the questions. Write your answers on the lines.

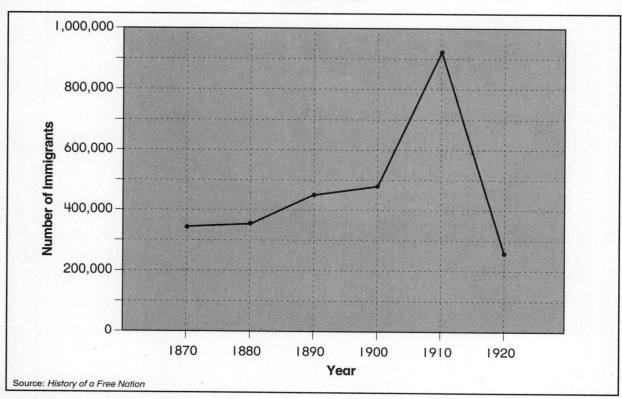

6. In which year did the largest number of Europeans immigrate to the United States?   **1910**

7. In which year were there about 440,000 European immigrants?   **1890**

8. In which ten-year period did the number of European immigrants increase most?   **1900 – 1910**

9. In which ten-year period was the number of European immigrants about 350,000 each year?   **1870 – 1880**

10. Between which years did the number of European immigrants decrease?   **1910 – 1920**

Regions — Chapter 6

Name: _____ Date: _____

WRITING

Write a short paragraph to answer each question. If you need more room, continue writing on the back of this page.

1. Look at the graph. Do most families in the United States live in urban, suburban, or rural areas? Summarize the information in the graph as you answer the question.

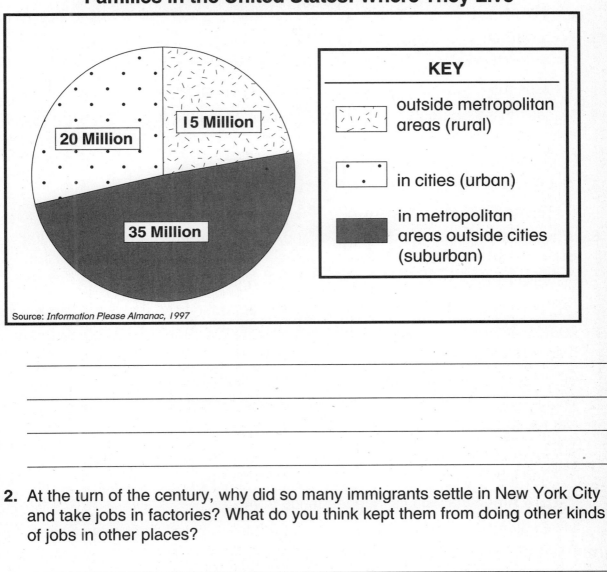

Families in the United States: Where They Live

Source: *Information Please Almanac*, 1997

_____
_____
_____
_____

2. At the turn of the century, why did so many immigrants settle in New York City and take jobs in factories? What do you think kept them from doing other kinds of jobs in other places?

_____
_____
_____
_____

Regions — Chapter 6

Name: _____   Date: _____

CONTENT AND SKILLS

Fill in the circle before the correct answer.

1. Who was the Mohawk leader who convinced Iroquois groups to form a confederacy?
   - ⓐ Onondaga
   - ⓑ Hiawatha
   - ⓒ Sequoyah
   - ⓓ Seneca

2. Members of the Grand Council of the Iroquois Confederacy were called _____.
   - ⓐ Huron
   - ⓑ Oneida
   - ⓒ unions
   - ⓓ sachems

3. Who warned Massachusetts colonists of an attack by British troops?
   - ⓐ Paul Revere
   - ⓑ Crispus Attucks
   - ⓒ George Washington
   - ⓓ Henry Longfellow

4. Massachusetts patriots who trained themselves to fight the British were known as _____.
   - ⓐ Pilgrims
   - ⓑ Regulars
   - ⓒ Minutemen
   - ⓓ Redcoats

5. The first battle of the American Revolution took place in _____.
   - ⓐ Boston
   - ⓑ Yorktown
   - ⓒ Philadelphia
   - ⓓ Lexington

6. Where was the first stop for many of the immigrants who came to the United States between 1890 and 1914?
   - ⓐ Ellis Island
   - ⓑ Washington, D.C.
   - ⓒ Lexington
   - ⓓ Chesapeake Bay

7. Many immigrants who settled in New York City lived in poorly built apartment buildings called _____.
   - ⓐ longhouses
   - ⓑ sweatshops
   - ⓒ tenements
   - ⓓ pushcarts

8. Many people moved to cities during the Industrial Revolution because they wanted to _____.
   - ⓐ start farms
   - ⓑ find jobs
   - ⓒ work on ships
   - ⓓ join an army

9. In 1816 Argentina won its independence from _____.
   - ⓐ England
   - ⓑ Spain
   - ⓒ France
   - ⓓ the United States

10. How are Argentina and the Northeastern region of the United States alike?
    - ⓐ Most people speak Spanish.
    - ⓑ Both have small populations.
    - ⓒ Both depend mainly on farming.
    - ⓓ Most people live in cities.

Regions

Unit 3

CONTENT AND SKILLS

Write the word or words from the box that best complete each statement.

| rivers | broadleaf and needleleaf trees | seasons |
| bays and harbors | Appalachian Mountains | |

11. _____ have helped make the Northeast an important fishing region.

12. The climate of the Northeast supports the growth of _____.

13. The first factories in the Northeast were built along the _____.

14. The _____ were shaped by glaciers thousands of years ago.

15. The _____ are more varied in the Northeast than in regions closer to the equator.

Write a term from the box to complete each sentence.

| global grid | circle graph | longitude | line graph | latitude |

16. A _____ shows how the parts of something make up a whole.

17. You can use a _____ to find the location of any place in the world.

18. Lines of _____ are used to measure distance east and west of the prime meridian.

19. A _____ shows how a piece of information changes over time.

20. Lines of _____ are used to measure distance north and south of the equator.

Name: _____   Date: _____

WRITING

Write a short paragraph to answer each question. If you need more room, continue writing on the back of this page.

1. Look at the map below. Which parts of the Northeast do you think tourists would most likely visit in autumn to see the trees change colors? Tell why you think so.

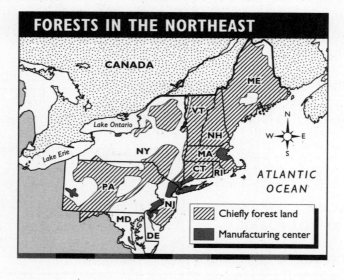

_____
_____
_____
_____
_____

2. Is your community urban, suburban, or rural? Do you think the population of your community will grow a lot in the future? Explain why or why not.

_____
_____
_____
_____
_____
_____
_____

Name: _____ Date: _____

CONTENT

Fill in the circle before the correct answer.

1. What is one reason why the Middle West is very cold in winter?
   - (a) Cold winds from the Atlantic blow across its plains.
   - (b) There are no mountains to block the movement of cold air.
   - (c) The lake effect from the Great Lakes makes winters chilly.
   - (d) Most of the land is below sea level and therefore cold.

2. Poland and the Interior Plains of the United States are alike because they _____.
   - (a) have many large cities
   - (b) are industrial areas
   - (c) have mostly flat farmland
   - (d) have few modern machines

3. Where are the largest deposits of iron found in the Middle West?
   - (a) Minnesota   (b) Nebraska   (c) Indiana   (d) Iowa

4. Most iron in the Middle West is mined by _____.
   - (a) digging deep tunnels
   - (b) heating rocks
   - (c) bulldozing open pits
   - (d) using giant magnets

5. Between 1880 and 1910 the demand for steel jumped because _____.
   - (a) most of the iron in the United States had been mined
   - (b) steel was easy and safe to manufacture
   - (c) steel was easier to mine than iron
   - (d) steel was needed to make cars, bridges, and buildings

Read each sentence and write the letter of the area it describes.

A. Great Plains   **B.** Central Plains   **C.** Great Lakes

6. _____ The climate is milder here because the land is near water.
7. _____ This part of the Interior Plains is low, with gentle hills.
8. _____ This part of the Interior Plains is mostly dry grassland.
9. _____ Wheat is the major crop in this region.
10. _____ Corn is the major crop in this region.

Regions   Chapter 7

Name: _____ Date: _____

SKILLS

Use the maps and a ruler or scale strip to answer each question.

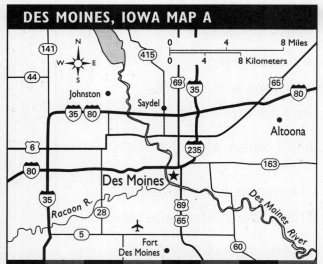
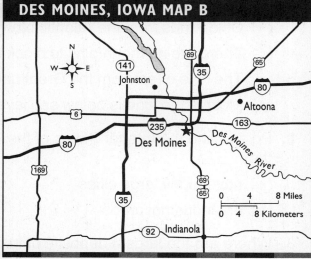

1. On which map does one inch represent a greater distance?
   _____

2. Which map would you use to find the distance between Johnston and Saydel?
   _____

3. Which map shows more details of the Des Moines area?
   _____

4. Look at Map A. What is the distance between Des Moines and Altoona?
   _____

5. Look at Map B. How far is Des Moines from Johnston?
   _____

Name: _____ Date: _____

WRITING

Write a short paragraph to answer each question. If you need more room, continue writing on the back of this page.

1. How do conditions in the Middle West make work both easier and harder for farmers?

   _____
   _____
   _____
   _____

2. Steel production has long been important to the economy of the Middle West. Look at the chart showing steel production during two periods of United States history. What happened to production between 1891 and 1910? What happened to production in more recent years? Explain your answers.

U.S. Steel Production

YEAR	PRODUCTION (IN TONS)
1891	4,349
1900	11,227
1910	28,330
1980	111,835,000
1987	89,151,000
1994	100,613,000

Sources: *Statistical Abstract of the United States*, 1995
American Iron and Steel Institute

_____
_____
_____
_____

Name: _____   Date: _____

CONTENT

Fill in the circle before the correct answer.

1. Many immigrants pushed west because land on the Atlantic Coast was _____.
   - (a) too moist for farming
   - (b) costly
   - (c) owned by the government
   - (d) not available

2. Pioneers were able to farm the prairies of the Interior Plains by use of the _____.
   - (a) combine
   - (b) Tin Lizzie
   - (c) Conestoga wagon
   - (d) steel plow

3. The life of the Lakota in the 1700s was changed by the arrival of the _____.
   - (a) dog
   - (b) buffalo
   - (c) horse
   - (d) deer

4. In the early 1900s many African Americans moved north in the _____.
   - (a) Great Migration
   - (b) mass production
   - (c) Westward Movement
   - (d) assembly line

5. Why do some farmers work directly with food-processing companies?
   - (a) The companies lend the farmers money.
   - (b) The agreement guarantees a good harvest.
   - (c) The farmer controls how the crops are packaged into food.
   - (d) The companies guarantee the farmer a certain price for crops.

Read each sentence and write the name of the person it describes: John Deere, Henry Ford, George Custer, Abraham Lincoln, Jean Baptiste Point du Sable.

6. He led the United States Army attack on the Lakota at Little Bighorn. _____

7. He invented the steel plow. _____

8. He set up the French trading post that later became the city of Chicago. _____

9. He was the future President whose family moved from Kentucky to the Indiana frontier. _____

10. He was the businessman whose switch to mass production made his cars popular and affordable. _____

Regions   Chapter 8

Name: _____ Date: _____

SKILLS

Use the three sets of dictionary guide words to answer questions 1–2.

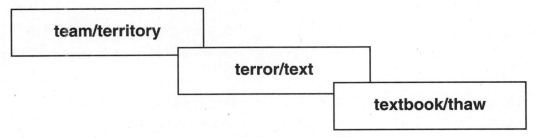

1. Under which set of guide words would you find the definition for the word **teepee**? _____

2. Under which set would you find the definition for **thatch**? _____

Use the encyclopedia volumes to answer questions 3–5.

3. In which volume should you look for information about Sitting Bull? _____

4. In which volume should you look for information about Abraham Lincoln? _____

5. In which volume should you look for information about the Cree Indians? _____

WRITING

Write a short paragraph to answer each question. If you need more room, continue writing on the back of this page.

1. In 1868 the Lakota and the United States government signed a treaty. The Lakota moved to a reservation that included the Black Hills. Part of the Treaty of 1868 said:

   > No white person or persons shall be permitted to settle upon or occupy any portion of the territory, or without the consent of the Indians to pass through the same.

   Source: *Bury My Heart at Wounded Knee*
   by Dee Brown, Holt, Rhinehart & Winston, 1970

   Before long, white settlers began moving through Lakota territory. Why were settlers interested in the Black Hills, and what was the result of their interest?

   _____
   _____
   _____
   _____
   _____
   _____
   _____

2. How has agriculture changed in the Middle West in recent years? What hasn't changed about it over the years?

   _____
   _____
   _____
   _____
   _____
   _____
   _____
   _____

Name: _____ Date: _____

CONTENT AND SKILLS

Fill in the circle before the correct answer.

1. What is the major crop on the Great Plains?
   - (a) rice
   - (b) wheat
   - (c) potatoes
   - (d) corn

2. Which resource is found in the Mesabi Range of Minnesota?
   - (a) gold
   - (b) coal
   - (c) silver
   - (d) iron

3. In which area is corn the main crop?
   - (a) Central Plains
   - (b) Appalachian Mountains
   - (c) Great Lakes
   - (d) Rocky Mountains

4. Which process involves clearing all the plants and soil away from an area and then digging ore out of the ground?
   - (a) large-scale agriculture
   - (b) open-pit mining
   - (c) mass production
   - (d) reclamation

5. Which part of the Middle West is affected by the "lake effect"?
   - (a) Nebraska
   - (b) Kansas
   - (c) western Illinois
   - (d) southern Michigan

6. The Great Plains area is mostly _____.
   - (a) moist farmland
   - (b) hilly prairie
   - (c) high mountains
   - (d) dry grassland

7. Which European country was the first to claim lands in the Middle West?
   - (a) France
   - (b) England
   - (c) Spain
   - (d) Germany

8. What happened when settlers tried to take over the part of the Lakota reservation known as the Black Hills in the 1870s?
   - (a) The Lakota moved away.
   - (b) The settlers returned home.
   - (c) War broke out.
   - (d) The settlers moved north.

9. In which city did Henry Ford and many other auto makers set up factories around 1900?
   - (a) Chicago
   - (b) New York
   - (c) Detroit
   - (d) Philadelphia

10. Turning crops into packaged food items sold in grocery stores is called _____.
    - (a) food processing
    - (b) mass production
    - (c) agribusiness
    - (d) breadbasket

Regions

Unit 4

CONTENT AND SKILLS

Write a term from the box to answer each question.

combine	mall	scale strip	CD-ROM
drought	steel plow	guide words	mass production
buffalo	map scale		

11. Farmers in the Middle West sometimes suffer from a long period of little or no rain, known as a _____.

12. Because of the harsh Middle Western winters, developers in Edina, Minnesota, built a _____ for shopping indoors.

13. The relationship between the distance shown on a map and the real distance on Earth is known as the _____.

14. To measure the distance between two points on a map accurately, you can take a piece of paper with a straight edge and make a _____.

15. In the 1830s a blacksmith named John Deere made it possible to farm the prairies by inventing the _____.

16. The Lakota traveled across the Great Plains in search of _____.

17. The process of manufacturing large numbers of goods by using identical parts is known as _____.

18. When using a dictionary, you can quickly figure out which page a word appears on by looking at the top of the page and checking the _____.

19. A compact disc that you can read with a computer is a _____.

20. The piece of farm equipment that both cuts and threshes wheat is a _____.

Name: _____   Date: _____

WRITING

Write a short paragraph to answer each question. If you need more room, continue writing on the back of this page.

1. How are the Central Plains and the Great Plains alike? How are they different? Compare and contrast the land and water, the climate, and the major crops grown in each region.

   _____
   _____
   _____
   _____
   _____

2. Look at the chart below. It shows changes in the number of people living on farms in the Middle Western state of Nebraska between 1910 and 1969. It also shows changes in the total population of the state. What do you think happened to the farm population? Explain.

Year	1910	1930	1950	1969
* Farm Population	631,000	587,000	391,000	263,000
** Total Population	1,192,214	1,377,963	1,325,510	(1970) 1,485,333

* Source: *Historical Statistics of the United States: Colonial Times to 1970*, U.S. Department of Commerce
** Source: *The World Almanac and Book of Facts*, 1995

   _____
   _____
   _____
   _____
   _____
   _____

Regions   Unit 4

Name: _____   Date: _____

CONTENT

Fill in the circle before the correct answer.

1. The process of water, wind, and ice slowly carrying away rock and soil is known as _____.
   - (a) refinement
   - (b) adaptation
   - (c) erosion
   - (d) drought

2. An aquifer is a source of _____.
   - (a) water
   - (b) plastic
   - (c) oil
   - (d) copper

3. By definition the amount of rain that falls each year in a desert is less than _____.
   - (a) 25 in.
   - (b) 20 in.
   - (c) 15 in.
   - (d) 10 in.

4. What was one cause of the Dust Bowl of the 1930s?
   - (a) There was a sudden, huge rise in the population of the Great Plains.
   - (b) Farmers in the Great Plains stopped growing wheat.
   - (c) Oil wells destroyed valuable farmland.
   - (d) Farmers had plowed up prairie grasses by planting wheat.

5. Like the Southwestern United States, Nigeria has grown rapidly as a result of _____.
   - (a) agriculture
   - (b) tourism
   - (c) petroleum
   - (d) manufacturing

Write the name of the place from the box that each sentence describes.

| Sonoran Desert | Texas | Tulsa | Grand Canyon | Houston |

6. This deep, narrow valley stretches 217 miles through northern Arizona. _____

7. Giant cactus trees called saguaros grow in this area in Arizona. _____

8. Patillo Higgins discovered oil in this state in 1901. _____

9. Today this city is our nation's top oil-refining center. _____

10. In 1905 a drilling crew found oil near this city in Oklahoma. _____

Regions   1   Chapter 9

SKILLS

Read the passage. Then write your answer to each question.

    The Grand Canyon is the most spectacular sight in the world. More than four million people visit it each year. Most tourists visit the south rim of the canyon. They should visit the north rim instead. The north rim is 1,200 feet higher than the south rim. The view from the north rim is very exciting.
    The south rim has many restaurants and viewing spots complete with telescopes. All of the tourist attractions ruin the experience of visiting the canyon. You will appreciate it most if you go to a quiet spot on the north rim and just admire the view.

Write three sentences from the passage that state opinions.

1. _____

2. _____

3. _____

Write two sentences from the passage that state facts.

4. _____

5. _____

Name: _____ Date: _____

WRITING

Write a short paragraph to answer each question. If you need more room, continue writing on the back of this page.

1. Look at the map of the Southwest. It shows some of the major industries in each state.

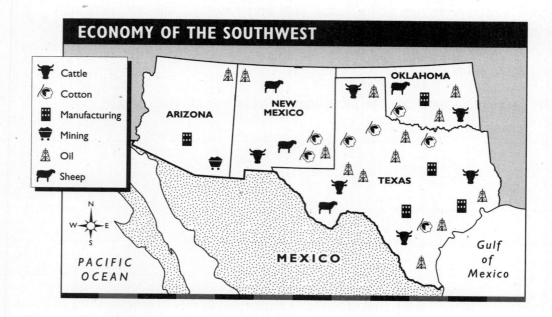

   How do people in other parts of the United States depend on the economy of the Southwest? Use examples from the map to explain.

   _____
   _____
   _____
   _____

2. Discuss the natural advantages and disadvantages of the Southwest. Give at least one example of each.

   _____
   _____
   _____
   _____
   _____

Name: _____ Date: _____

CONTENT

Fill in the circle before the correct answer.

1. By the early 1600s the Navajo survived mainly by _____.
   - (a) hunting
   - (b) herding
   - (c) farming
   - (d) mining

2. Who was Manuelito?
   - (a) a Spanish conquistador
   - (b) a Spanish vaquero
   - (c) an African scout
   - (d) a Navajo leader

3. In 1821 the Southwest became _____.
   - (a) part of Mexico
   - (b) part of Spain
   - (c) an independent nation
   - (d) part of the United States

4. Which invention meant the end of the long cattle drives?
   - (a) the truck
   - (b) barbed wire
   - (c) the brand
   - (d) the computer

5. What was manufactured in the Southwest in the 1940s?
   - (a) computers
   - (b) cameras
   - (c) weapons
   - (d) spacecraft

Write the name from the box that best fits each description.

| Santa Fe   Dinetah   Window Rock   Kitt Peak   Sun Belt |

6. This city in Arizona is the Navajo capital. _____

7. This city was the capital of the Spanish colony of New Mexico. _____

8. This is a name for the Navajo reservation. _____

9. This part of the United States has a warm, sunny climate all or most of the year. _____

10. This place in Arizona is home to the largest solar telescope in the world. _____

Regions   1   Chapter 10

Name: _____   Date: _____

SKILLS

Read the two passages below. Then write your answer to each question.

A

On warm moonlit nights as I rode around the herd, I would say to myself, "This is the life!" My horse seemed to understand my thoughts, and to share my feeling. I always picked the best horse in my string for my night animal, and used him whenever I had to night herd. He and I became real friends.

—James Cook

Source: *Cowboys of the Wild West* by Russell Freedman, Clarion Books, New York, 1985

B

The ranch a cowboy worked for usually gave him a "string" of six or eight horses to use. Cowboys worked their horses hard and often had to change mounts several times a day. As a result, the cowboy got to know their different personalities and abilities. When a cowboy had to herd cattle at night, he would pick the horse that had the best eyesight and sense of direction.

—Stacey Sparks

1. Is selection A a primary or secondary source?
   _____

2. What kind of source is selection B?
   _____

3. What helped you decide what kind of source selection A is?
   _____

4. What helped you decide what kind of source selection B is?
   _____
   _____

5. Which selection gives you a better understanding of a cowboy's feelings for his horse? Tell why.
   _____
   _____

Name: _____   Date: _____

WRITING

Write a short paragraph to answer each question. If you need more room, continue writing on the back of this page.

1. Read the chart below. What does it show about the climate of the Southwest compared with the climate in other parts of the country? Use the chart to help explain how the climate has affected the population of the region in both the past and the present.

STATE	AVERAGE NUMBER OF SUNNY DAYS PER YEAR	AVERAGE TEMPERATURE IN JULY (°F)
Arizona	310	94
New Mexico	277	79
Oklahoma	248	82
Texas	248	83
Nebraska	219	77
Maine	208	69
Ohio	186	72
Washington	183	65

Sources: U.S. Department of Commerce, *World Almanac and Books of Facts,* 1995

_____
_____
_____
_____

2. What traditions are still practiced by the Navajo community today? Give at least two examples.

_____
_____
_____
_____

Name: _____ Date: _____

CONTENT AND SKILLS

Fill in the circle before the correct answer.

1. What kind of statement can be proven true?
   - (a) opinion
   - (b) fact
   - (c) belief
   - (d) feeling

2. What happened after United States soldiers shot a herd of horses that belonged to the Navajo leader Manuelito?
   - (a) War broke out.
   - (b) The Navajo invaded New Mexico.
   - (c) Mexico invaded Texas.
   - (d) A peace treaty was made.

3. The Navajo march from Fort Defiance, Arizona, to Fort Sumner, New Mexico, was called the _____.
   - (a) Trail of Tears
   - (b) mission
   - (c) Long Walk
   - (d) conquistador

4. Coronado explored the Southwest in search of _____.
   - (a) salt
   - (b) horses
   - (c) iron
   - (d) gold and silver

5. What river flows through the Grand Canyon?
   - (a) Mississippi
   - (b) Rio Grande
   - (c) Missouri
   - (d) Colorado

6. Texas leads the nation in _____.
   - (a) producing copper
   - (b) making electrical devices
   - (c) raising cattle and sheep
   - (d) attracting tourists

7. Which natural resource is being used a great deal in Phoenix, Arizona, because of the city's large rise in population?
   - (a) water
   - (b) soil
   - (c) sun
   - (d) minerals

8. What kind of industry is growing rapidly in Phoenix?
   - (a) farming
   - (b) high technology
   - (c) logging
   - (d) food processing

9. A diary written by someone who took part in an event that he or she is describing is an example of _____.
   - (a) fact
   - (b) primary source
   - (c) belief
   - (d) secondary source

10. Which invention helped bring more people to the Southwest earlier in this century?
    - (a) telephone
    - (b) computer
    - (c) television
    - (d) air conditioning

Regions   1   Unit 5

CONTENT AND SKILLS

Choose the word from the box that best fits each description. Write the word on the line.

dry farming	butte	hogan	vaquero
aquifer	feedlot	refinery	mission
petroleum	drought		

11. a landform that looks like a small hill with a flat top　_____

12. a way to grow crops with only rainwater　_____

13. a period of little or no rain　_____

14. an underground layer of rock or gravel that traps water　_____

15. a major Southwestern resource that was formed underground from dead plants over millions of years　_____

16. a factory where crude oil is turned into usable products　_____

17. a traditional Navajo home　_____

18. a Christian settlement built by the Spanish　_____

19. a large pen for cattle　_____

20. one of the first North American cowboys　_____

Name: _____ Date: _____

WRITING

Write a short paragraph to answer each question. If you need more room, continue writing on the back of this page.

1. How has the environment of the Southwest affected the population of the region?

   _____
   _____
   _____
   _____
   _____
   _____

2. Look at the map of Spanish settlements in the Southwest in the 1600s and 1700s. Describe the kinds of settlements the Spanish built in the Southwest at that time.

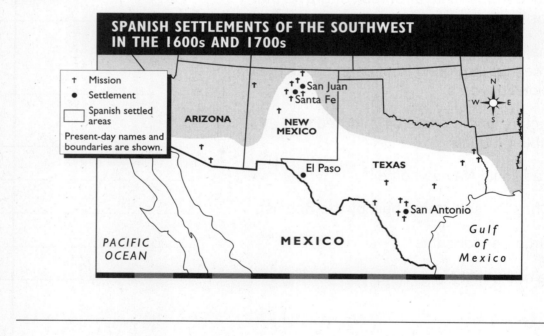

   _____
   _____
   _____
   _____
   _____

CONTENT

Fill in the circle before the correct answer.

1. What problem used to make farming difficult in the Central Valley of California?
   - (a) little rainfall
   - (b) steep hillsides
   - (c) poor soil
   - (d) cold weather

2. What happens at the highest elevations in the Rocky Mountains?
   - (a) Spruce trees grow taller.
   - (b) Temperatures are high.
   - (c) Trees become twisted and bent.
   - (d) Only grass and lichens survive.

3. What is deforestation?
   - (a) the moving of forests from one area to another
   - (b) the loss of whole forests
   - (c) the harvesting of one kind of tree
   - (d) the process of removing dead or burnt trees from an area

4. Which of the following is characteristic of rain forests?
   - (a) bright, sunny weather
   - (b) strong winds
   - (c) humid air
   - (d) little wildlife

5. Latex is a rain forest product used to make _____.
   - (a) medicine
   - (b) food
   - (c) fabric
   - (d) rubber

Write the letter of the place next to each description.

a. Olympia National Park	d. Death Valley, California
b. Sacramento River	e. Sierra Nevada
c. Amazon River	

6. _____ This mountain range marks the eastern border of California.

7. _____ This is the driest place in the United States.

8. _____ This national park in the state of Washington has several rain forest areas.

9. _____ This river in Brazil is the world's second longest.

10. _____ This river flows through the northern part of California's Central Valley.

Regions   Chapter 11

Name:	Date:

SKILLS

Look at the map of Redding, California, and the surrounding area. Use the map to write the answer to each question.

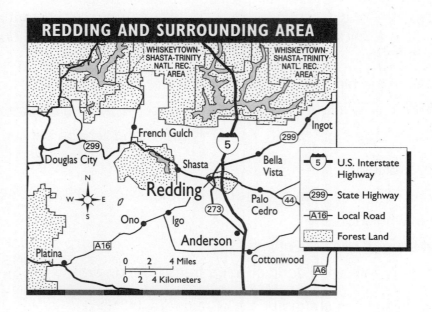

1. Draw an arrow to point to the interstate highway on this map.

2. What kind of road goes from Ono to Redding?
   _____

3. What kind of road connects Platina and Ono on this map?
   _____

4. What road goes from Shasta to Douglas City?
   _____

5. What kind of road is the road from Shasta to Douglas City?
   _____

Regions — Chapter 11

Name: _____   Date: _____

WRITING

Write a short paragraph to answer each question. If you need more room, continue writing on the back of this page.

1. What are some of the different products you and your family use that are made from trees? Give some examples and tell why it is important to use our forest resources wisely.

   _____
   _____
   _____

2. Look at the map of the West. Use the map to help explain why the West is considered a "land of extremes."

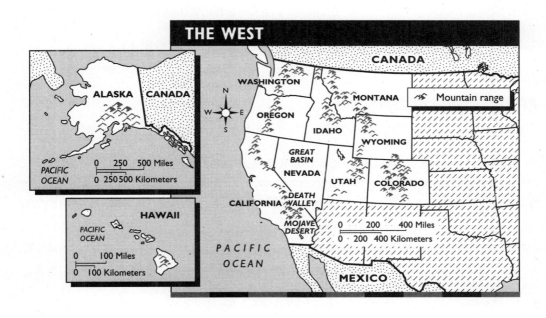

   _____
   _____
   _____
   _____
   _____

Regions   Chapter 11

Name: _____ Date: _____

CONTENT

Fill in the circle before the correct answer.

1. The first people who settled in the Hawaiian islands were probably the _____.
   - (a) Inuit
   - (b) Ute
   - (c) Polynesians
   - (d) Shoshoni

2. What happened to James Cook, the first European explorer to reach Hawaii?
   - (a) He united the eight islands.
   - (b) He started a pineapple plantation.
   - (c) He made Hawaii a part of the United States.
   - (d) He was killed in a fight while visiting the islands.

3. In 1848 thousands of people rushed to California to _____.
   - (a) grow sugarcane
   - (b) cut sandalwood
   - (c) look for gold
   - (d) make movies

4. The women's suffrage movement was a fight for the right to _____.
   - (a) vote
   - (b) own land
   - (c) immigrate
   - (d) mine gold

5. Japan has to import most of its _____.
   - (a) computers
   - (b) televisions
   - (c) automobiles
   - (d) raw materials

Write the letter of the person or place beside each description.

a. San Francisco	c. Los Angeles	e. Susan B. Anthony
b. Liliuokalani	d. Pike's Peak	

6. _____ When gold was found here, thousands of people moved to Colorado.

7. __a__ In the middle 1800s many Chinese flocked to this American city, creating a neighborhood still known as Chinatown.

8. _____ She was the last queen of Hawaii.

9. _____ She met Elizabeth Cady Stanton in Seneca Falls and joined her to fight for women's suffrage.

10. _____ This California city is home to the movie and television industries.

Regions   Chapter 12

SKILLS

Read the statements below. Then follow the instructions.

- Melissa's ancestors moved to California because their tiny farm in China could not produce enough food for them.
- Anne's ancestors migrated to Hawaii in the 1900s because of political problems in their homeland of Germany.

1. Write a generalization based on these statements about why many people moved to the Western United States.

   _____

   _____

2. Write a second generalization about where the people now living in the West originally came from.

   _____

   _____

- Mark's grandfather immigrated to Oregon because he couldn't find a job in Japan for someone with his education.
- Anchee's Chinese ancestors immigrated to Alaska to prospect for gold during the Alaska gold rush.

3. Write a generalization based on these statements about why many people moved to the West.

   _____

   _____

4. Write a second generalization about where the people now living in the West originally came from.

   _____

   _____

5. Write a generalization about immigration to the United States based on all of the statements above.

   _____

   opportunities.

Regions   Chapter 12

Name: _____   Date: _____

WRITING

Write a short paragraph to answer each question. If you need more room, continue writing on the back of this page.

1. The Declaration of Independence states, "All men are created equal." The declaration from the women's rights convention of 1848 by Elizabeth Cady Stanton and Lucy Mott states, "We hold these truths to be self-evident: that all men and women are created equal."

   How did this belief lead to major changes in the United States, and what were some of the major events in the history of the suffrage movement in the West?

   _____
   _____
   _____
   _____

2. The time line below shows when certain groups of people arrived in the Hawaiian islands. How did the arrival of each group change Hawaii?

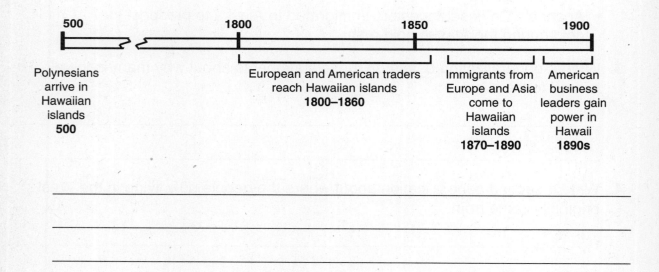

   _____
   _____
   _____
   _____

Name: _____ Date: _____

CONTENT AND SKILLS

Fill in the circle before the correct answer.

1. Turpentine, rayon, and paper are all made from _____.
   - (a) rubber
   - (b) wood
   - (c) cotton
   - (d) leaves

2. The act of destroying an entire forest is called _____.
   - (a) logging
   - (b) erosion
   - (c) strip mining
   - (d) deforestation

3. Which kind of road connects two or more states?
   - (a) local road
   - (b) interstate highway
   - (c) state highway
   - (d) toll road

4. Which interstate road probably runs east-west?
   - (a) Route 91
   - (b) Route 15
   - (c) Route 10
   - (d) Route 1

5. If you are hiking in the mountains and you walk up to higher and higher elevations, the _____.
   - (a) temperature will drop
   - (b) precipitation will increase
   - (c) temperature will rise
   - (d) pollution will increase

6. The dry side of a mountain range lies in an area known as the _____.
   - (a) lake effect
   - (b) rain shadow
   - (c) desert
   - (d) coastal plain

7. Elizabeth Cady Stanton and Susan B. Anthony traveled throughout the West making speeches in favor of _____.
   - (a) slavery
   - (b) industry
   - (c) war
   - (d) women's suffrage

8. California was an ideal location for filming movies because of its _____.
   - (a) population
   - (b) farming
   - (c) climate
   - (d) natural resources

9. A sentence that states what is similar about several different examples is _____.
   - (a) a generalization
   - (b) a supporting statement
   - (c) an opinion
   - (d) a fact

10. Japan must import most of its _____.
    - (a) automobiles
    - (b) workers
    - (c) food
    - (d) raw materials

Regions

Unit 6

Name: _____ Date: _____

CONTENT AND SKILLS

Choose the term or name from the box that best fits each description. Write the choice on the line.

Chico Mendes	Central Valley Project	Queen Liliuokalani
Coast Ranges	transcontinental railroad	Thomas Edison
Polynesia	California Gold Rush	Brazil
ghost town		

11. mountains in western California that overlook the Pacific Ocean _____

12. the irrigation system that made California one of our nation's largest producers of fruits and vegetables _____

13. a huge group of islands that include the Hawaiian islands _____

14. the Hawaiian ruler who was overthrown in 1893 by a group of business leaders _____

15. an event that began in 1848 with the discovery of gold at Sutter's Mill _____

16. a place that was abandoned after the gold had run out _____

17. completed on May 8, 1869, in Promontory Point, Utah _____

18. the inventor who played an important part in improving movie cameras _____

19. where most of the Amazon River basin lies _____

20. the rubber tapper who died trying to save the Brazilian rain forest _____

Regions   Unit 6

WRITING

Write a short paragraph to answer each question. If you need more room, continue writing on the back of this page.

1. Look at the two tables below.

LUMBER USED IN THE UNITED STATES (millions of board feet)		
1985	**1990**	**1995**
53,468	54,482	58,543

Source: U.S. Bureau of the Census

LUMBER PRODUCED IN THE WESTERN UNITED STATES (billions of board feet)		
1985	**1990**	**1995**
19.3	21.6	15.9

Source: U.S. Bureau of the Census

What do these tables show? How does this information affect the economy of the West? Think about where lumber comes from and the effects of cutting more and more trees.

_____
_____
_____
_____

2. In what ways are the United States and Japan interdependent? Be sure to name what products are traded between the United States and Japan.

_____
_____
_____
_____

Regions — Unit 6

Part 4

Performance Assessment

Chapter 1 .... T31
Chapter 2 .... T34
Unit 1 .... T37
Chapter 3 .... T38
Chapter 4 .... T41
Unit 2 .... T44
Chapter 5 .... T45
Chapter 6 .... T48
Unit 3 .... T51
Chapter 7 .... T52
Chapter 8 .... T55
Unit 4 .... T58
Chapter 9 .... T59
Chapter 10 .... T62
Unit 5 .... T65
Chapter 11 .... T66
Chapter 12 .... T69
Unit 6 .... T72

Performance Assessment

Chapter 1: Writing a Description

Goal
The student will demonstrate knowledge of landforms and climate by writing a description of the local area.

Suggestions:
1. Bring in and share an article or travel description of the local area's landforms and climate and have students brainstorm a list of landforms.
2. Model the process by giving an example description of a landform in the local area and/or a list of annual weather statistics.

Portfolio Opportunities
Have students evaluate their own paragraphs by telling what they like best about them. Then have students collect their paragraphs in a notebook or place them in their portfolios.

SCORING RUBRIC

4 An **excellent** paragraph describes at least three landforms and two aspects of climate. The description uses strong visual language and presents information in a logical order. Landforms might include mountains, hills, plains, plateaus, and basins. Descriptions of climate might include average temperatures and average precipitation at different times of the year. The paragraph is written with correct use of conventions (grammar, punctuation, capitalization, and spelling).

3 A **good** paragraph describes two kinds of landforms and two aspects of climate. The description uses strong visual language and presents information in a logical order. The paragraph is written with generally correct use of conventions.

2 A **fair** paragraph describes two kinds of landforms and two aspects of climate. The description may not use particularly strong visual language and may not present information in a logical order. The paragraph may include some errors in the use of conventions.

1 A **poor** paragraph may describe a landform or some aspect of climate but does not include both, or it may list features rather than describe them.

0 An **unscorable** paragraph is unreadable or does not relate to the task.

Performance Assessment

Chapter 1: Writing an Advertisement

Goal
The student shows an awareness of the importance of conserving resources by designing and writing an advertisement.

Suggestions:
1. Have students choose a resource described in Lesson 3 and brainstorm ideas for conserving the resource.
2. Model the process by bringing in and sharing an advertisement or a poster designed to encourage conservation of a resource.

Portfolio Opportunities
Have students exchange ads with their partners and evaluate them by completing peer assessment checklists. Then have students display their ads and place the peer assessment checklists in their portfolios.

SCORING RUBRIC

4 An **excellent** advertisement uses strong illustrations or other visuals and concise text to encourage people to conserve a natural resource, such as water, clean air, forests, food sources, minerals, or fuel. The advertisement has at least three good ideas for conserving the resource. The text of the advertisement is written with correct use of conventions (grammar, punctuation, capitalization, and spelling).

3 A **good** advertisement uses strong illustrations or other visuals and concise text to encourage people to conserve a natural resource. The advertisement has two good ideas for conserving the resource. The text of the advertisement is written with generally correct use of conventions.

2 A **fair** advertisement uses an illustration or other visual and concise text to encourage people to conserve a natural resource. The advertisement has one good idea for conserving the resource. The text of the advertisement may include some errors in the use of conventions.

1 A **poor** advertisement does not have a visual, does not include text describing ideas for conserving a resource, or does not present accurate information about conservation.

0 An **unscorable** advertisement is incomplete, it is not presented as an ad, or it does not relate to conserving resources.

Performance Assessment

Chapter 1: Writing an Explanation

Goal
The student will write a paragraph explaining factors that influence climate in different parts of the country.

Suggestions:
1. Review Lesson 2 and have students discuss the factors that influence climate.

2. Model the process by explaining how one particular factor affects climate in your area.

Portfolio Opportunities
Have students evaluate their own paragraphs by completing self-assessment checklists. Then have students place their paragraphs and self-assessments in their portfolios.

SCORING RUBRIC

4 An **excellent** explanation presents specific information about three factors that influence climate in at least three different parts of the country. The information is presented in a logical order. Factors that influence climate should include distance from the ocean, distance from the equator, and elevation. Parts of the country may include regions (Southeast, Northwest, etc.), states, or specific areas (such as the Rocky Mountains or Coastal Plain). The text is written with correct use of conventions (grammar, punctuation, capitalization, and spelling).

3 A **good** explanation presents specific information about two factors that influence climate in two different parts of the country. The information is presented in a logical order. The text is written with generally correct use of conventions.

2 A **fair** explanation presents specific information about two factors that influence climate in at least one part of the country. The information may not be presented in a logical order. The text may include some errors in the use of conventions.

1 A **poor** paragraph does not present specific information about factors that influence climate or does not explain how those factors influence the climate in a specific area.

0 An **unscorable** paragraph is incomplete or is not related to climate.

Performance Assessment

Chapter 2: Writing a Description

Goal
The student will show an awareness of customs by writing a description of a custom.

Suggestions:
1. Have students define *custom* and discuss how their families celebrate a particular holiday, such as Thanksgiving.
2. Model the process by describing how you and your family celebrate a particular holiday.

Portfolio Opportunities
Have students exchange descriptions with their partners and evaluate the descriptions by completing peer assessment checklists. Then have students display their descriptions or place them in their portfolios with the peer assessment checklists.

SCORING RUBRIC

4 An **excellent** paragraph describes at least four characteristics or features of a particular custom. The description uses strong visual language and presents information in a logical order. Customs might include celebrating a holiday, such as Thanksgiving, Kwanzaa, or Hanukkah. Characteristics or features might include foods, dances, music, clothing, or activities associated with the custom. The paragraph is written with correct use of conventions (grammar, punctuation, capitalization, and spelling).

3 A **good** paragraph describes three characteristics or features of a particular custom. The description uses strong visual language and presents information in a logical order. The paragraph is written with generally correct use of conventions.

2 A **fair** paragraph describes two characteristics or features of a particular custom. The description may not use particularly strong visual language and may not present information in a logical order. The paragraph may include some errors in the use of conventions.

1 A **poor** paragraph may mention a custom or a holiday but does not describe its characteristics or features.

0 An **unscorable** paragraph is unreadable or does not relate to the task.

Performance Assessment

Chapter 2: Writing an Explanation

Goal
The student will write a paragraph explaining ideas to include in a constitution for a new country.

Suggestions:
1. Review Lesson 2 and have students discuss the purpose and contents of the United States Constitution.
2. Model the process by summarizing or describing the basic principles of our Constitution.

Portfolio Opportunities
Have students evaluate their own paragraphs by completing self-assessment checklists. Then have students place their paragraphs and self-assessments in their portfolios.

SCORING RUBRIC

4 An **excellent** explanation presents at least four specific principles or ideas that would be included in a constitution for a new country. The information is presented in a logical order, and the paragraph clearly conveys the idea that a constitution is a plan for a government. Principles or ideas might include branches of government, who leads the government, how laws are made, and how laws are enforced. The paragraph might also describe the type of government, such as a representative democracy. The text is written with correct use of conventions (grammar, punctuation, capitalization, and spelling).

3 A **good** explanation presents three specific principles or ideas that would be included in a constitution for a new country. The information is presented in a logical order, and the paragraph clearly conveys the idea that a constitution is a plan for a government. The text is written with generally correct use of conventions.

2 A **fair** explanation presents two specific principles or ideas that would be included in a constitution for a new country. The information may not be presented in a logical order, or the paragraph may not clearly convey the idea that a constitution is a plan for a government. The text may include some errors in the use of conventions.

1 A **poor** paragraph does not present specific principles or ideas for a constitution and does not convey the idea that a constitution is a plan for a government.

0 An **unscorable** paragraph is incomplete or is not related to the task.

Performance Assessment

Chapter 2: Writing a Newspaper Article

Goal
The student will write a news article about the students who started the business called Food From the 'Hood.

Suggestions:
1. Review Lesson 3 in the chapter and discuss the steps the students took in developing their business.
2. Model the process by bringing in and sharing a news article on how another business got started.

Portfolio Opportunities
Have students work in small groups to present their news articles and complete peer assessment checklists to evaluate one another's work. Then have students place their articles in their portfolios with the peer assessment checklists.

SCORING RUBRIC

4 An **excellent** news article tells who, what, when, where, and why in a logical order with correct use of conventions (grammar, punctuation, capitalization, and spelling). It describes at least four major steps in the development of Food From the 'Hood. Steps might include thinking of the idea for salad dressing, finding investment money, creating and testing the product, manufacturing, packaging, getting the product into the stores, accounting, and transportation.

3 A **good** news article reflects four of the 5 Ws in a logical order with generally correct use of conventions (grammar, punctuation, capitalization, and spelling). It describes three major steps in the development of Food From the 'Hood.

2 A **fair** news article reflects two or three of the 5 Ws in a logical order. It describes two major steps in the development of Food From the 'Hood. The text may include some errors in the use of conventions.

1 A **poor** news article may describe the product or the company in a general way, but it does not describe who, when, where, or why.

0 An **unscorable** news article is unreadable or has nothing to do with Food From the 'Hood.

Performance Assessment

Unit 1 Review Project: Make a Geography Mobile

Goal
The student will demonstrate knowledge of the geography and resources of North America by working with a group to construct a mobile.

Suggestions:
1. Have students brainstorm a list of natural resources and features as a step in designing the mobile and encourage students in each group to cover as much of the geography and resources of North America as they can in one mobile.
2. Model the process by making or bringing in a mobile about another subject or topic.

Portfolio Opportunities
Have students exchange their mobiles with other groups and evaluate them by using the questions on the peer assessment checklist. For individual assessment have each student complete a self-assessment checklist to evaluate his or her contribution to the project.

SCORING RUBRIC

4 An **excellent** mobile includes at least eight geographic features and/or resources representing different parts of the country. For example, features might include the Appalachian Mountains, Rocky Mountains, Mississippi River, Coastal Plain, Interior Plains. Resources might include water, air, soil, forests, people. Each shape in the mobile is presented with colorful decoration or creative ideas, and it has a clear, concise caption to identify it. The text is written with correct use of conventions (grammar, punctuation, capitalization, and spelling).

3 A **good** mobile includes six or seven geographic features and/or resources representing different parts of the country. Each shape in the mobile has a caption, but the shape may not be presented in a creative or artistic way. The text is written with generally correct use of conventions.

2 A **fair** mobile includes four or five geographic features and/or resources, but they may not represent several different parts of the country. Each shape in the mobile has a caption, but the shape may not be presented in a creative or artistic way. The text may include some errors in the use of conventions.

1 A **poor** mobile includes one or two geographic features and one or two resources. The features and resources do not represent all parts of the country. The shapes and resources in the mobile may not be labeled, or the captions may not be clear and concise.

0 An **unscorable** mobile is incomplete, is not presented as a mobile, or has nothing to do with geographic features and resources.

Performance Assessment

Chapter 3: Writing an Explanation

Goal
The student will explain the importance of the Mississippi River by writing a paragraph.

Suggestions:
1. Review Lesson 1 and have students discuss the Mississippi River basin.
2. Model the process by displaying a map of the United States and describing the size of the area drained by the Mississippi River and its tributaries.

Portfolio Opportunities
Have students evaluate their own paragraphs by completing self-assessment checklists. Then have students place their paragraphs and self-assessments in their portfolios.

SCORING RUBRIC

4 An **excellent** explanation presents at least four specific pieces of information to support Mark Twain's statement that "the basin of the Mississippi is the body of the nation." The information is presented in a logical order, and it conveys the idea that a basin is all the land that is drained by a river and its tributaries. Information might include these facts: the source of the Mississippi River is in Minnesota, and the river flows into the Gulf of Mexico; the river and its tributaries drain land in 31 states and two Canadian provinces; its tributaries reach into all five regions of the United States. The text is written with correct use of conventions (grammar, punctuation, capitalization, and spelling).

3 A **good** explanation presents three specific pieces of information to support Mark Twain's statement that "the basin of the Mississippi is the body of the nation." The information is presented in a logical order, and it conveys the idea that a basin is all the land that is drained by a river and its tributaries. The text is written with generally correct use of conventions.

2 A **fair** explanation presents two specific pieces of information to support Mark Twain's statement that "the basin of the Mississippi is the body of the nation." The information may not be presented in a logical order, and it may not clearly convey the idea that a basin is all the land that is drained by a river and its tributaries. The text may include some errors in the use of conventions.

1 A **poor** paragraph does not present specific information and does not convey the idea that a basin is all the land that is drained by a river and its tributaries.

0 An **unscorable** paragraph is incomplete or is not related to the Mississippi River.

Performance Assessment

Chapter 3: Writing a Letter

Goal
The student describes some of the sights in the Southeast in a friendly letter.

Suggestions:
1. Review the Infographic in the chapter and have students brainstorm a list of sights in the Southeast.
2. Model the process by writing and sharing a brief letter describing the sights in your own community to a friend or colleague who lives in another community.

Portfolio Opportunities
Have students evaluate their own letters by completing a self-assessment checklist. Then have students display their letters and place their self-assessments in their portfolios.

SCORING RUBRIC

4 An **excellent** letter describes at least five sights in the Southeast. For example, the letter might describe the Great Smoky Mountains, the Okefenokee Swamp, the Everglades, the Mississippi River, the Piedmont, beaches on the Gulf of Mexico and the Atlantic Ocean, coal mines, farms that grow peanuts, cotton, rice, or tobacco, and citrus groves. The letter includes all the parts of a letter (date, salutation, body, closing, and signature), and the information in the letter is presented in a logical order. The text is written with correct use of conventions (grammar, punctuation, capitalization, and spelling).

3 A **good** letter describes four sights in the Southeast. The letter includes all the parts of a letter (date, salutation, body, closing, and signature), and the information in the letter is presented in a logical order. The text is written with generally correct use of conventions.

2 A **fair** letter describes three sights in the Southeast. The letter includes at least three of the parts of a letter (date, salutation, body, closing, and signature). The information in the letter may not be presented in a logical order. The text may include some errors in the use of conventions.

1 A **poor** letter describes only one or two sights in the Southeast, or it does not include the parts of a letter.

0 An **unscorable** letter is unreadable, is not written as a letter, or does not have anything to do with the Southeast.

Performance Assessment

Chapter 3: Writing a Summary

Goal
The student describes the climate, growing season, and crops of the Southeast by writing a summary of Lesson 2.

Suggestions:
1. Review Lesson 2 and have students determine the most important pieces of information to include in a summary.
2. Model the process by writing and/or reading aloud a paragraph describing another region or another aspect of the Southeast.

Portfolio Opportunities
Have students exchange summaries with their partners and evaluate them by completing peer assessment checklists. Then have students collect their summaries in a notebook or place them in their portfolios with the peer assessment checklists.

SCORING RUBRIC

4 An **excellent** summary has a strong topic sentence and three or more detail sentences that condense the most important information from the lesson. For example, the summary might state that the Southeast has a fairly warm climate with adequate precipitation, and it has a long growing season. Important crops include oranges, peanuts, rice, cotton, and tobacco. The text is written with correct use of conventions (grammar, punctuation, capitalization, and spelling).

3 A **good** summary has a topic sentence and two or more detail sentences that condense the most important information from the lesson. Details include three important crops. The text is written with generally correct use of conventions.

2 A **fair** summary has a topic sentence and two detail sentences that present information from the lesson and mention two important crops. The topic sentence may not be clear, and some of the details may not represent the most important information from the lesson. The text may include some errors in the use of conventions.

1 A **poor** summary does not have a topic sentence, it does not describe the climate and the growing season, or it does not mention important crops grown in the Southeast.

0 An **unscorable** summary is incomplete or is not related to the Southeast.

Performance Assessment

Chapter 4: Writing an Alphabet

Goal
The student will demonstrate the concept of an alphabet by inventing ten new letters in the alphabet and writing a coded message.

Suggestions:
1. Review the Cherokee alphabet given in Lesson 1 and discuss which letters in the English alphabet are used most often.
2. Model the process by inventing new symbols for ten letters in the alphabet and writing a coded message.

Portfolio Opportunities
Have students exchange coded messages with partners and write a sentence describing what they like best about the partner's alphabet. Then have students display their messages or place them in their portfolios with partners' comments included.

SCORING RUBRIC

4 An **excellent** message is written in code and explains something the student learned in the chapter. The code has invented symbols for ten of the letters in the English alphabet, and the message uses the symbols accurately and consistently. The decoded text is written with correct use of conventions (grammar, punctuation, capitalization, and spelling).

3 A **good** message is written in code and explains something the student learned in the chapter. The code has invented symbols for ten of the letters in the English alphabet, and the message uses the symbols accurately and consistently. The decoded text is written with generally correct use of conventions.

2 A **fair** message is written in code, although it may not explain something the student learned in the chapter. The code has invented symbols for ten of the letters in the English alphabet, but the message may not use the symbols accurately and consistently. The decoded text may include some errors in the use of conventions.

1 A **poor** message is not written in code or does not use symbols for letters accurately or consistently.

0 An **unscorable** message is unreadable or does not relate to the task.

Performance Assessment

Chapter 4: Writing an Interview

Goal
The student writes an interview with Harriet Tubman.

Suggestions:
1. Review the information on Harriet Tubman in Lesson 3 and discuss the kinds of questions one might ask her about her life and what she did.
2. Model the process by having students ask you questions about how you became a teacher.

Portfolio Opportunities
Have students evaluate their own interviews by using them to role-play with partners and discussing what is good about them and what might be improved. Then have students share their interviews with the class and place the interviews in their portfolios.

SCORING RUBRIC

4 An **excellent** interview has three well-written questions and a specific response to each question. The questions are easy to understand, are specific to Tubman's life, lead to informative responses, and are presented in a logical sequence. At least one of the questions focuses on the Underground Railroad. The responses are appropriate to the questions and provide accurate information about Tubman. The text is written with correct use of conventions (grammar, punctuation, capitalization, and spelling).

3 A **good** interview has three well-written questions and a specific response to each question. The questions are specific to Tubman, lead to informative responses, and are presented in a logical sequence. At least one of the questions focuses on the Underground Railroad. The responses are appropriate to the questions and provide accurate information about Tubman, although they may not be as complete as they could be. The text is written with generally correct use of conventions.

2 A **fair** interview has two well-written questions and a specific response to each question. The interview may include other questions that are not appropriate or are not well written, and it may include some inaccurate information in the responses. At least one of the questions mentions the Underground Railroad. The text may include some errors in the use of conventions.

1 A **poor** interview does not have clear, focused questions and does not lead to informative responses.

0 An **unscorable** interview is unreadable, is not written as an interview, or does not have anything to do with Harriet Tubman.

Performance Assessment

Chapter 4: Writing a Summary

Goal
The student summarizes the major events in the colonies from 1774 to 1776.

Suggestions:
1. Review Lesson 2 and have students determine the most important events to include in a summary of the years 1774 to 1776.
2. Model the process by writing and/or reading aloud a paragraph summarizing another period in history or the most important events in the last year.

Portfolio Opportunities
Have students exchange summaries with their partners and evaluate them by completing peer assessment checklists. Then have students collect their summaries in a notebook or place them in their portfolios with the peer assessment checklists.

SCORING RUBRIC

4 An **excellent** summary has a strong topic sentence and three or more detail sentences that describe at least four major events in the colonies in the years 1774 to 1776. For example, the summary might discuss the growing anger of the colonists against England, Jefferson's statement that "British Parliament has no right to exercise authority over us," the breaking up of the House of Burgesses, the meeting of the Continental Congress, the decision to break free of England, the Declaration of Independence, and the beginning of the war with England. The text is written with correct use of conventions (grammar, punctuation, capitalization, and spelling).

3 A **good** summary has a topic sentence and two or more detail sentences that describe three major events in the years 1774 to 1776. The text is written with generally correct use of conventions.

2 A **fair** summary has a topic sentence and two detail sentences that describe two major events in the years 1774 to 1776. The topic sentence may not be clear, and some of the details may not represent the most important information from the lesson. The text may include some errors in the use of conventions.

1 A **poor** summary does not have a topic sentence or does not describe more than one event in the years 1774 to 1776.

0 An **unscorable** summary is incomplete or is not related to the colonies in 1774 to 1776.

Performance Assessment

Unit 2 Review Project: Design Southeast Maps

Goal

The student will demonstrate an understanding of how the economy of the Southeast has shifted from mostly agriculture to mostly manufacturing by designing and creating maps of the Southeast.

Suggestions:

1. Have students review Chapter 3 and discuss evidence of the change in the economy of the Southeast.
2. Model the process by making or bringing in a map of your state showing some of its products.

Portfolio Opportunities

Have students exchange maps with partners and evaluate the maps by using the questions on the peer assessment checklist. Then have students display their maps and place the peer assessments in their portfolios.

SCORING RUBRIC

4 An **excellent** project includes two maps of the Southeast that are labeled "Before 1900" and "After 1900." Each map has at least four pictures of products made or grown in the Southeast. The pre-1900 map reflects mostly agriculture, and the post-1900 map reflects mostly manufacturing. Each picture clearly depicts the subject, and each map is generally accurate in shape and detail. The text is written with correct use of conventions (grammar, punctuation, capitalization, and spelling).

3 A **good** project includes two maps of the Southeast that are labeled "Before 1900" and "After 1900." Each map has three pictures of products made or grown in the Southeast. The pre-1900 map reflects mostly agriculture, and the post-1900 map reflects mostly manufacturing. Each picture clearly depicts the subject, and each map is generally accurate in shape and detail. The text is written with generally correct use of conventions.

2 A **fair** project includes two maps of the Southeast that are labeled "Before 1900" and "After 1900." Each map has two pictures of products made or grown in the Southeast, although the maps may also include pictures that do not reflect accurate information. The pre-1900 map reflects mostly agriculture, and the post-1900 map reflects mostly manufacturing. The maps may include some errors in shape and detail, and the text may include some errors in the use of conventions.

1 A **poor** project has only one map, it has only one picture of a product on each of two maps, or it depicts inaccurate information about the Southeast.

0 An **unscorable** project is incomplete, is not presented as maps, or has nothing to do with products in the Southeast.

Performance Assessment

Chapter 5: Writing a Journal

Goal
The student will describe the Appalachian Trail in a journal entry.

Suggestions:
1. Bring in and share photographs of sights on the Appalachian Trail in the Northeast, or review pictures in the chapter, and discuss what hikers might see on the trail.
2. Model the process by describing some of the sights you have seen on a hike you have taken.

Portfolio Opportunities
Have students exchange journal entries with partners and write a sentence describing what they like best about the partner's journal entry. Then have students display their journal entries, with pictures of sights on the Appalachian Trail, or place them in their portfolios with partners' comments included.

SCORING RUBRIC

4 An **excellent** journal entry gives specific details about an imaginary hike on the Appalachian Trail, notes one or more specific days or dates, and includes personal observations describing four or more places or sights seen on the trip (for example, cornfields and barns in Pennsylvania, a small zoo in New York, old logging roads in the Green Mountains of Vermont, and Mount Katahdin in Maine). The journal entry is written with correct use of conventions (grammar, punctuation, capitalization, and spelling).

3 A **good** journal entry gives specific details about an imaginary hike on the Appalachian Trail, notes one or more specific days or dates, and includes personal observations describing three places or sights seen on the trip. The journal entry is written with generally correct use of conventions.

2 A **fair** journal entry gives some specific details about an imaginary hike on the Appalachian Trail and includes personal observations describing one or two places or sights seen on the trip. The journal entry may not include specific days or dates. It may include descriptions of places or sights that are not on the Appalachian Trail, and it may include some errors in the use of conventions.

1 A **poor** journal entry does not include specific details about an imaginary hike on the Appalachian Trail and does not describe places or sights.

0 An **unscorable** journal entry is unreadable or does not relate to the task.

Performance Assessment

Chapter 5: Writing a Poem

Goal
The student will describe autumn in the Northeast by writing a poem.

Suggestions:
1. Reread the Many Voices on page 153 and bring in and share some pictures or personal observations of autumn in the Northeast. Have students discuss what images autumn in the Northeast brings to mind.
2. Model the process by bringing in and sharing some poems (for example, from Robert Frost) describing autumn in the Northeast.

Portfolio Opportunities
Have students read their poems aloud to their partners and write a sentence describing what they like best about the partner's poem. Then have students display their poems, with pictures of autumn in the Northeast, or place them in their portfolios with partners' comments included.

SCORING RUBRIC

4   An **excellent** poem uses effective language to create strong visual images of autumn in the Northeast. It conveys a sense of change in the weather or the seasons as the leaves turn color and a sense of the beauty of the colors themselves. The poem may or may not use a specific rhyme scheme. The poem is written with correct use of conventions (grammar, punctuation, capitalization, and spelling).

3   A **good** poem uses language to create some images of autumn in the Northeast. It conveys a sense of change in the weather or the seasons as the leaves turn color. The poem may or may not use a specific rhyme scheme. The poem is written with generally correct use of conventions.

2   A **fair** poem has at least one visual image and describes some aspect of the changes that occur during autumn in the Northeast. The poem may or may not use a specific rhyme scheme. The poem may include some errors in the use of conventions.

1   A **poor** poem has no visual images or does not describe changes that occur during autumn in the Northeast.

0   An **unscorable** poem is incomplete or is not written as a poem.

Performance Assessment

Chapter 5: Writing an Explanation

Goal
The student will write a paragraph explaining longitude and latitude and why an understanding of longitude and latitude might be important to someone exploring an unknown place.

Suggestions:
1. Review the Skills Lesson in the chapter and have students discuss the uses of latitude and longitude.
2. Model the process by displaying a map of the United States and locating places by latitude and longitude.

Portfolio Opportunities
Have students evaluate their own paragraphs by completing self-assessment checklists. Then have students place their paragraphs and self-assessments in their portfolios.

SCORING RUBRIC

4 An **excellent** paragraph provides a clear explanation of latitude and longitude and explains how it would be helpful to a person exploring an unknown place. The information is presented in a logical order, and it conveys the idea that latitude and longitude can be used to locate places anywhere on Earth. The explanation might state that lines of latitude indicate the distance north or south of the equator, and lines of longitude indicate distance east or west of the prime meridian. These lines, measured in degrees, can be used to locate places. When exploring an unknown place, lines of latitude and longitude can be used to navigate or to find a specific place. The text is written with correct use of conventions (grammar, punctuation, capitalization, and spelling).

3 A **good** paragraph provides an explanation of latitude and longitude and explains how it would be helpful to a person exploring an unknown place. The information is presented in a logical order, and it conveys the idea that latitude and longitude can be used to locate places anywhere on Earth. The text is written with generally correct use of conventions.

2 A **fair** paragraph provides an explanation of latitude and longitude, and it conveys the idea that latitude and longitude can be used to locate places anywhere on Earth. The information may not be presented in a logical order. The text may include some errors in the use of conventions.

1 A **poor** paragraph does not explain latitude and longitude or how it might be helpful to a person exploring an unknown place.

0 An **unscorable** paragraph is incomplete or is not related to latitude and longitude.

Performance Assessment

Chapter 6: Writing an Explanation

Goal
The student will write a paragraph explaining how the Iroquois Confederacy helped bring strength and peace to its member groups.

Suggestions:
1. Review Lesson 1 and have students discuss the benefits brought about by the Iroquois Confederacy.
2. Model the process by writing and/or reading aloud an explanation of the benefits brought about by another organization (such as the United Nations or NATO).

Portfolio Opportunities
Have students evaluate their own paragraphs by completing self-assessment checklists. Then have students place their paragraphs and self-assessments in their portfolios.

SCORING RUBRIC

4 An **excellent** paragraph clearly explains at least three ways the Iroquois Confederacy brought strength and peace to its members. It presents some background information about the five member groups (Seneca, Cayuga, Onondaga, Oneida, and Mohawk) and how they lived before the Confederacy was formed, and it presents the information in a logical order. For example, the paragraph might explain that the five groups began fighting over resources, had disagreements among themselves, and fought with other groups (such as the Huron). The Iroquois Confederacy helped bring strength and peace to its members by providing a means for sharing resources, discussing trade, keeping peace among its members, resolving differences between and within member groups, and presenting a united front against other groups. The text is written with correct use of conventions (grammar, punctuation, capitalization, and spelling).

3 A **good** paragraph clearly explains two ways the Iroquois Confederacy brought strength and peace to its members. It presents some background information about the five member groups and how they lived before the Confederacy was formed, and it presents the information in a logical order. The text is written with generally correct use of conventions.

2 A **fair** paragraph explains one or two ways the Iroquois Confederacy brought strength and peace to its members. It may not include background information about the five member groups and may not present information in a logical order. The text may include some errors in the use of conventions.

1 A **poor** paragraph does not explain how the Iroquois Confederacy brought strength and peace to its members.

0 An **unscorable** paragraph is incomplete or is not related to the Iroquois Confederacy.

Performance Assessment

Chapter 6: Writing an Interview

Goal
The student writes an interview with an immigrant arriving at Ellis Island.

Suggestions:
1. Review the information on immigrants in Lesson 3 and discuss the kinds of questions one might ask an immigrant arriving in this country.
2. Model the process by playing the role of an immigrant and having students ask you questions about your experiences.

Portfolio Opportunities
Have students evaluate their own interviews by using them to role-play with partners and discussing what is good about them and what might be improved. Then have students share their interviews with the class and place the interviews in their portfolios.

SCORING RUBRIC

4 An **excellent** interview has at least three well-written questions and a specific response to each question. The questions are easy to understand, are specific to an immigrant's experience, lead to informative responses, and are presented in a logical sequence. At least one of the questions focuses on why the person came to the United States. The responses are appropriate to the questions and provide accurate information. The text is written with correct use of conventions (grammar, punctuation, capitalization, and spelling).

3 A **good** interview has two or three well-written questions and a specific response to each question. The questions are specific to an immigrant's experience, lead to informative responses, and are presented in a logical sequence. At least one of the questions focuses on why the person came to the United States. The responses are appropriate to the questions and provide accurate information, but they may not be as complete as they could be. The text is written with generally correct use of conventions.

2 A **fair** interview has one or two well-written questions and a specific response to each question. The interview may include other questions that are not appropriate or are not well written, and it may include some inaccurate information in the responses. At least one of the questions focuses on why the person came to the United States. The text may include some errors in the use of conventions.

1 A **poor** interview does not have clear, focused questions and does not lead to informative responses.

0 An **unscorable** interview is unreadable, is not written as an interview, or does not have anything to do with immigrants arriving at Ellis Island.

Performance Assessment

Chapter 6: Writing a Paragraph

Goal
The student will explain the causes and effects of the battles at Lexington and Concord by writing a paragraph.

Suggestions:
1. Review Lesson 2 and have students discuss the causes and effects of the battles at Lexington and Concord.
2. Model the process by displaying a cause-effect or by reading a cause-and-effect paragraph about a different event.

Portfolio Opportunities
Have students evaluate their own paragraphs by completing self-assessment checklists. Then have students place their paragraphs and self-assessments in their portfolios.

SCORING RUBRIC

4 An **excellent** paragraph clearly explains at least three causes and two effects of the battles at Lexington and Concord, and it presents the information in a logical order. For example, causes might include the colonists' resentment of British rule, their resentment toward Britain for having to pay unfair taxes, the colonists' boycott of British goods, the Boston Massacre, the closing of the port of Boston, and the British march on Lexington and Concord. Effects might include the beginning of the American Revolutionary War, the demonstration that the colonists intended to stage an armed rebellion, and ultimately the independence of the United States. The text is written with correct use of conventions (grammar, punctuation, capitalization, and spelling).

3 A **good** paragraph explains two causes and two effects of the battles at Lexington and Concord, and it presents the information in a logical order. The text is written with generally correct use of conventions.

2 A **fair** paragraph explains two causes and one effect of the battles at Lexington and Concord. It may not present the information in a logical order, and it may include some information that is not accurate. The text may include some errors in the use of conventions.

1 A **poor** paragraph may explain one cause or one effect of these battles, but not both.

0 An **unscorable** paragraph is incomplete or is not related to the battles at Lexington and Concord.

Performance Assessment

Unit 3 Review Project: Make a Growth Mural

Goal
The student will demonstrate an understanding of why cities in the Northeast have grown by working with a group to create a mural.

Suggestions:
1. Have students review Chapter 6, Lesson 4, and make a list of reasons to explain why cities of the Northeast have grown.
2. Model the process by giving an example of a reason for growth and showing a picture that represents the reason.

Portfolio Opportunities
Have students evaluate one another's murals by using the questions on the peer assessment checklist. Then have students display their murals and place the peer assessments in their portfolios. For individual assessment have each student complete a self-assessment checklist to evaluate his or her contribution to the project.

SCORING RUBRIC

4 An **excellent** mural presents at least four reasons to explain the growth of cities in the Northeast. Each reason is presented as a picture or drawing, and the mural is presented with colorful decoration or creative ideas. For example, reasons might include: the Industrial Revolution created a need for workers for factories in the cities; many of the immigrants who arrived in the United States settled in the cities of the Northeast; most Northeastern cities were busy ports and centers of trade, so they offered jobs; new modes of transportation made travel in and out of the cities easier, so the cities expanded. The text is written with correct use of conventions (grammar, punctuation, capitalization, and spelling).

3 A **good** mural presents three different reasons to explain the growth of cities in the Northeast. Each reason is presented as a picture or drawing, and the mural is presented with some form of decoration or creative ideas. The text is written with generally correct use of conventions.

2 A **fair** mural presents two different reasons to explain the growth of cities in the Northeast. Each reason is presented as a picture or drawing. The mural may include some pictures that do not reflect reasons for the cities' growth, and the text may include some errors in the use of conventions.

1 A **poor** mural has only one reason, although it may have more than one picture, or it depicts inaccurate information about the growth of cities in the Northeast.

0 An **unscorable** project is incomplete, is not presented as a mural, or has nothing to do with the growth of cities in the Northeast.

Performance Assessment

Chapter 7: Writing a Poem

Goal
The student will describe the plains in the 1800s by writing a poem.

Suggestions:
1. Reread the Many Voices on page 221 and bring in and share some pictures or personal observations of the plains. Have students discuss what images the plains bring to mind.
2. Model the process by bringing in and sharing some poems describing the plains.

Portfolio Opportunities
Have students read their poems aloud to their partners and write a sentence describing what they like best about the partner's poem. Then have students display their poems, with pictures of the plains, or place them in their portfolios with partners' comments included.

SCORING RUBRIC

4 An **excellent** poem uses effective language to create strong visual images of the plains in the 1800s. It conveys a sense of the vastness of the plains and their "lonely beauty." The poem may or may not use a specific rhyme scheme. The poem is written with correct use of conventions (grammar, punctuation, capitalization, and spelling).

3 A **good** poem uses language to create some images of the plains in the 1800s. It conveys a sense of vastness and beauty. The poem may or may not use a specific rhyme scheme. The poem is written with generally correct use of conventions.

2 A **fair** poem has at least one visual image and describes some aspect of the plains in the 1800s. The poem may or may not use a specific rhyme scheme. The poem may include some errors in the use of conventions.

1 A **poor** poem has no visual images or does not describe the plains in the 1800s.

0 An **unscorable** poem is incomplete or is not written as a poem.

Performance Assessment

Chapter 7: Writing a Comparison

Goal
The student will compare farming in Poland with farming in the Middle West by writing a comparison/contrast paragraph.

Suggestions:
1. Review the Global Connections lesson in the chapter and have students discuss how farming in Poland is similar to and different from farming in the Middle West.
2. Model the process by making a comparison/contrast chart or by reading aloud a comparison/contrast paragraph on a different subject.

Portfolio Opportunities
Have students evaluate their own paragraphs by telling what they like best about them. Then have students collect their paragraphs in a notebook or place them in their portfolios.

SCORING RUBRIC

4 An **excellent** paragraph has a main idea or topic sentence and three or more sentences with supporting details. The main idea or topic sentence clearly states a comparison of farming in Poland with farming in the Middle West. The rest of the paragraph gives comparisons and contrasts clearly identified as "alike" or "different." For example, the two areas are alike in that the land is flat, there are many farms, farmers grow some of the same crops, such as wheat, and farmers in both places use fertilizers and pesticides. Farming in Poland is different in that the land is not very fertile, most of the farms are rather small, and the farmers do not use as many modern machines as farmers in the Middle West. The paragraph is written with correct use of conventions (grammar, punctuation, capitalization, and spelling).

3 A **good** paragraph has a main idea or topic sentence and two sentences with supporting details. The main idea or topic sentence clearly states a comparison. The rest of the paragraph gives at least one comparison and one contrast clearly identified as "alike" or "different." The paragraph is written with generally correct use of conventions.

2 A **fair** paragraph has a main idea or topic sentence and at least one sentence with supporting details describing how farming in Poland is like or different from farming in the Middle West. The main idea or topic sentence may not state the comparison clearly. The supporting details may include information that is not clearly related to the main idea. The paragraph may include some errors in the use of conventions.

1 A **poor** paragraph does not have a main idea or topic sentence, or it does not have supporting details. The paragraph does not accurately compare and contrast farming in Poland and farming in the Middle West.

0 An **unscorable** paragraph is incomplete or is not presented as a paragraph of comparison.

Performance Assessment

Chapter 7: Writing an Article

Goal
The student will write a news article about the construction of the first skyscraper in Chicago in 1883.

Suggestions:
1. Bring in and share pictures of early skyscrapers and discuss with students what an impression these first buildings must have made on people who had never seen tall buildings.
2. Model the process by bringing in and sharing a news article on the construction of a building or other similar event.

Portfolio Opportunities
Have students work in small groups to present their news articles and complete peer assessment checklists to evaluate one another's work. Then have students place their articles in their portfolios with the peer assessment checklists.

SCORING RUBRIC

4 An **excellent** news article tells who, what, when, where, and why in a logical order with correct use of conventions (grammar, punctuation, capitalization, and spelling). It describes some aspects of how the building was constructed (with a steel frame) and gives an impression of how amazed people were to see such a tall building.

3 A **good** news article reflects four of the 5 Ws in a logical order with generally correct use of conventions (grammar, punctuation, capitalization, and spelling). It describes some aspects of how the building was constructed (with a steel frame) and gives an impression of how amazed people were to see such a tall building.

2 A **fair** news article reflects two or three of the 5 Ws in a logical order. It describes some aspect of how the building was constructed (with a steel frame) or gives an impression of how amazed people were to see such a tall building. The text may include some errors in the use of conventions.

1 A **poor** news article may describe the building in a general way, but it does not describe who, when, where, or why.

0 An **unscorable** news article is unreadable or has nothing to do with the construction of a skyscraper in Chicago in 1883.

Performance Assessment

Chapter 8: Writing a Journal Entry

Goal
The student will describe traveling westward by Conestoga wagon in a journal entry.

Suggestions:
1. Review the Many Voices journal entry and discuss what travelers might have seen and done on their journey westward.
2. Model the process by pointing out the characteristics of the journal entry by Jane Voorhees Lewis.

Portfolio Opportunities
Have students exchange journal entries with partners and write a sentence describing what they like best about the partner's journal entry. Then have students display their journal entries, with pictures of scenes during the westward movement, or place them in their portfolios with partners' comments included.

SCORING RUBRIC

4 An **excellent** journal entry gives specific details about an imaginary trip westward in a Conestoga wagon, notes one or more specific days or dates, and includes at least four personal observations describing places or sights seen on the trip, daily activities, or the appearance of the wagon. For example, the journal entry might describe the slow pace of travel, the use of mules, oxen, or horses to pull the wagon, its resemblance to a "prairie schooner," or the flatness of the prairie. The journal entry is written with correct use of conventions (grammar, punctuation, capitalization, and spelling).

3 A **good** journal entry gives specific details about an imaginary trip westward in a Conestoga wagon, notes one or more specific days or dates, and includes three personal observations describing places or sights seen on the trip, daily activities, or the appearance of the wagon. The journal entry is written with generally correct use of conventions.

2 A **fair** journal entry gives some specific details about an imaginary trip westward in a Conestoga wagon and includes personal observations describing one or two places or sights seen on the trip. The journal entry may not include specific days or dates. It may include descriptions of places or sights that would not have been on the prairie at the time, and it may include some errors in the use of conventions.

1 A **poor** journal entry does not include specific details about an imaginary trip westward and does not describe places or sights.

0 An **unscorable** journal entry is unreadable or does not relate to the task.

Performance Assessment

Chapter 8: Writing an Interview

Goal
The student will write an interview with Sitting Bull in the 1870s at the time of the discovery of gold in the Black Hills.

Suggestions:
1. Review the information on Sitting Bull in Lesson 2 and discuss the kinds of questions one might ask him at the time when gold was discovered in the Black Hills.
2. Model the process by playing the role of a settler or a Lakota of the time and having students ask you questions about your experiences.

Portfolio Opportunities
Have students evaluate their own interviews by using them to role-play with partners and discussing what is good about them and what might be improved. Then have students share their interviews with the class and place the interviews in their portfolios.

SCORING RUBRIC

4 An **excellent** interview has at least three well-written questions and a specific response to each question. The questions are easy to understand, are specific to Sitting Bull and the situation at the time, lead to informative responses, and are presented in a logical sequence. At least one of the questions focuses on Sitting Bull's refusal to give up the Black Hills or his role in the battle of Little Bighorn. The responses are appropriate to the questions and provide accurate information. The text is written with correct use of conventions (grammar, punctuation, capitalization, and spelling).

3 A **good** interview has two or three well-written questions and a specific response to each question. The questions are specific to Sitting Bull and the situation at the time, lead to informative responses, and are presented in a logical sequence. At least one of the questions focuses on Sitting Bull's refusal to give up the Black Hills or his role in the battle of Little Bighorn. The responses are appropriate to the questions and provide accurate information, but they may not be as complete as they could be. The text is written with generally correct use of conventions.

2 A **fair** interview has one or two well-written questions and a specific response to each question. The interview may include other questions that are not appropriate or are not well written, and it may include some inaccurate information in the responses. At least one of the questions focuses on Sitting Bull's refusal to give up the Black Hills or his role in the battle of Little Bighorn. The text may include some errors in the use of conventions.

1 A **poor** interview does not have clear, focused questions and does not lead to informative responses.

0 An **unscorable** interview is unreadable, is not written as an interview, or does not have anything to do with Sitting Bull.

Performance Assessment

Chapter 8: Writing an Explanation

Goal
The student will write a paragraph explaining how technology has changed the way a family farm is run today.

Suggestions:
1. Review Lesson 4 and have students discuss some of the changes in family farms brought about by technology.
2. Model the process by writing and/or reading aloud an explanation of how technology has changed the way you live or the way you work.

Portfolio Opportunities
Have students evaluate their own paragraphs by completing self-assessment checklists. Then have students place their paragraphs and self-assessments in their portfolios.

SCORING RUBRIC

4 An **excellent** paragraph clearly explains at least three ways in which technology has changed the way family farms are run today, and it presents the information in a logical order. For example, the paragraph might explain that many farmers now use huge combines to harvest crops, keep track of crops on a computer, get higher yields from today's seeds, work closely with food processing companies to sell their crops, and store grain in a grain elevator. The text is written with correct use of conventions (grammar, punctuation, capitalization, and spelling).

3 A **good** paragraph explains two ways in which technology has changed the way family farms are run today, and it presents the information in a logical order. The text is written with generally correct use of conventions.

2 A **fair** paragraph explains one or two ways in which technology has changed the way family farms are run today. It may not present the information in a logical order. The text may include some errors in the use of conventions.

1 A **poor** paragraph does not explain how technology has changed the way family farms are run today, or it presents inaccurate information.

0 An **unscorable** paragraph is incomplete or is not related to technology and farming.

Performance Assessment

Unit 4 Review Project: Make a Reclamation Flow Chart

Goal

The student will demonstrate an understanding of the land reclamation process by making a flow chart.

Suggestions:

1. Have students review Lesson 3 and make a list of the steps in a land reclamation project.
2. Model the process by showing an example of a flow chart describing another process or activity.

Portfolio Opportunities

Have students exchange flow charts with partners and evaluate the flow charts by completing peer assessment checklists. Then have students display their flow charts and place the peer assessments in their portfolios.

SCORING RUBRIC

4 An **excellent** flow chart shows four steps in land reclamation: (1) the effects of open-pit mining, (2) reshaping the land with machinery, (3) replanting grass and other plants, and (4) the same piece of land looking like a farm or a park. Each step is presented as a picture or drawing in correct sequence, and an explanation is provided on a separate piece of paper. The explanation describes the steps accurately and clearly. The text is written with correct use of conventions (grammar, punctuation, capitalization, and spelling).

3 A **good** flow chart shows three steps in land reclamation. Each step is presented as a picture or drawing in correct sequence, and an explanation is provided on a separate piece of paper. The explanation describes the steps accurately and clearly. The text is written with generally correct use of conventions.

2 A **fair** flow chart shows the two most important steps in land reclamation. Each step is presented as a picture or drawing in correct sequence, and an explanation is provided on a separate piece of paper. The explanation may not be clear, or the steps may not be described in correct sequence. The text may include some errors in the use of conventions.

1 A **poor** flow chart has only one step, it does not include an explanation, or it depicts inaccurate information.

0 An **unscorable** project is incomplete, is not presented as a flow chart, or has nothing to do with land reclamation.

Performance Assessment

Chapter 9: Writing a List

Goal

The student makes a list of five vocabulary words from Chapter 9 and writes a sentence using each of them.

Suggestions:

1. Review the vocabulary words in the chapter.
2. Model the process by using some of the words in sentences.

Portfolio Opportunities

Have students exchange lists with partners and evaluate the sentences by completing peer assessment checklists. Then have students place the lists in their portfolios with the peer assessments.

SCORING RUBRIC

4   An **excellent** list gives five vocabulary words from the chapter and uses all five words in well-written sentences. The use of each word in a sentence reflects an accurate understanding of it and its relation to the content of the chapter. The sentences are written with correct use of conventions (grammar, punctuation, capitalization, and spelling).

3   A **good** list gives five vocabulary words from the chapter and uses four of them accurately in sentences that reflect an understanding of the words and their relation to the content of the chapter. The sentences are written with generally correct use of conventions.

2   A **fair** list gives five vocabulary words from the chapter and uses three of them accurately in sentences that reflect an understanding of the words and their relation to the content of the chapter. The sentences may include some errors in the use of conventions.

1   A **poor** list gives five or fewer than five vocabulary words from the chapter and uses two or fewer of them accurately in sentences.

0   An **unscorable** list is incomplete or does not give the vocabulary words from the chapter.

Performance Assessment

Chapter 9: Writing an Article

Goal
The student will write a travel article about a trip to the Grand Canyon.

Suggestions:
1. Bring in and share pictures of the Grand Canyon and have students discuss what they might see if they went there.
2. Model the process by bringing in and sharing a travel article about a national park or similar destination.

Portfolio Opportunities
Have students work in small groups to present their travel articles and complete peer assessment checklists to evaluate one another's work. Then have students place their articles in their portfolios with the peer assessment checklists.

SCORING RUBRIC

4 An **excellent** travel article tells who, what, when, where, and why in a logical order with correct use of conventions (grammar, punctuation, capitalization, and spelling). It describes some of the sights and activities a visitor would see or take part in on a trip to the Grand Canyon, such as hiking down from the South Rim, viewing the canyon from a helicopter, camping in the canyon, or riding the rapids on a raft. The article also gives a brief explanation of how the Grand Canyon was formed.

3 A **good** travel article reflects four of the 5 Ws in a logical order with generally correct use of conventions. It describes some of the sights and activities a visitor would see or take part in on a trip to the Grand Canyon and gives a brief explanation of how the Grand Canyon was formed.

2 A **fair** travel article reflects two or three of the 5 Ws in a logical order. It describes some of the sights and activities a visitor would see or take part in on a trip to the Grand Canyon, but it may not explain how the Grand Canyon was formed. The text may include some errors in the use of conventions.

1 A **poor** travel article may describe the Grand Canyon in a general way, but it does not describe who, when, where, or why.

0 An **unscorable** travel article is unreadable or has nothing to do with the Grand Canyon.

Performance Assessment

Chapter 9: Writing a Letter

Goal
The student writes a friendly letter to a pen pal in Lagos, Nigeria.

Suggestions:
1. Review the Global Connections lesson in the chapter and have students brainstorm a list of questions they might ask of a pen pal in Lagos, Nigeria.
2. Model the process by writing and sharing a brief letter that asks questions about what life is like in a particular foreign country.

Portfolio Opportunities
Have students evaluate their own letters by completing a self-assessment checklist. Then have students display their letters and place their self-assessments in their portfolios.

SCORING RUBRIC

4 An **excellent** letter has at least four well-written questions about life in Lagos. The questions reflect an awareness that Lagos is a large, busy, crowded city. The letter includes all the parts of a letter (date, salutation, body, closing, and signature), and the questions in the letter are presented in a logical order. The text is written with correct use of conventions (grammar, punctuation, capitalization, and spelling).

3 A **good** letter has three well-written questions about life in Lagos. The questions reflect an awareness that Lagos is a large, busy, crowded city. The letter includes all the parts of a letter (date, salutation, body, closing, and signature), and the questions in the letter are presented in a logical order. The text is written with generally correct use of conventions.

2 A **fair** letter has two well-written questions about life in Lagos. The questions reflect an awareness that Lagos is a large, busy, crowded city. The letter includes at least three of the parts of a letter (date, salutation, body, closing, and signature). The questions in the letter may not be presented in a logical order. The text may include some errors in the use of conventions.

1 A **poor** letter has only one question or none, it does not reflect an awareness that Lagos is a large, busy, crowded city, or it does not include the parts of a letter.

0 An **unscorable** letter is unreadable, is not written as a letter, or does not have anything to do with life in Lagos.

Performance Assessment

Chapter 10: Writing an Explanation

Goal
The student will write a paragraph explaining how too much growth can cause problems in an area such as Phoenix.

Suggestions:
1. Review Lesson 4 and have students discuss some of the problems caused by the growth of cities in the desert, such as Phoenix.
2. Model the process by writing and/or reading aloud an explanation of how growth has caused some problems in your community or a nearby city.

Portfolio Opportunities
Have students evaluate their own paragraphs by completing self-assessment checklists. Then have students place their paragraphs and self-assessments in their portfolios.

SCORING RUBRIC

4 An **excellent** paragraph clearly explains at least four problems caused by too much growth in areas such as Phoenix, and it presents the information in a logical order. For example, the paragraph might explain that too much growth in an area such as Phoenix puts a strain on resources, especially water; creates an increased demand for air conditioning, which requires more electricity; requires more pavement, which raises the temperature of the city; and increases the population, which leads to more cars and more traffic congestion. The text is written with correct use of conventions (grammar, punctuation, capitalization, and spelling).

3 A **good** paragraph explains three problems caused by too much growth in areas such as Phoenix, and it presents the information in a logical order. The text is written with generally correct use of conventions.

2 A **fair** paragraph explains two problems caused by too much growth in areas such as Phoenix. It may not present the information in a logical order. The text may include some errors in the use of conventions.

1 A **poor** paragraph does not explain how too much growth causes problems in areas such as Phoenix, or it presents inaccurate information.

0 An **unscorable** paragraph is incomplete or is not related to problems caused by growth.

Performance Assessment

Chapter 10: Writing a Paragraph

Goal
The student will compare Navajo daily life during the 1600s with Navajo life today by writing a paragraph.

Suggestions:
1. Review Lesson 1 and have students discuss how Navajo life in the 1600s differed from Navajo life today.
2. Model the process by making a comparison/contrast chart or by reading aloud a comparison/contrast paragraph on a different subject.

Portfolio Opportunities
Have students exchange paragraphs with their partners and evaluate the paragraphs by completing peer assessment checklists. Then have students collect their paragraphs in a notebook or place them in their portfolios with the peer assessments.

SCORING RUBRIC

4 An **excellent** paragraph has a main idea or topic sentence and three or more sentences with supporting details. The main idea or topic sentence clearly states a comparison of Navajo life in the 1600s and today. The rest of the paragraph gives at least two comparisons and two contrasts clearly identified as "alike" or "different." For example, in the 1600s many Navajo lived in hogans, depended on sheep herding for food and wool, grew corn, and practiced traditional arts such as weaving. Today many Navajo still raise sheep, and they also raise cattle. Many live in hogans, but others live in modern houses. Mineral resources found on the reservation have provided a source of income for the Navajo, and many Navajo work in factories. Many Navajo still practice traditional arts such as weaving. The paragraph is written with correct use of conventions (grammar, punctuation, capitalization, and spelling).

3 A **good** paragraph has a main idea or topic sentence and two sentences with supporting details. The main idea or topic sentence clearly states a comparison. The rest of the paragraph gives at least one comparison and one contrast clearly identified as "alike" or "different." The paragraph is written with generally correct use of conventions.

2 A **fair** paragraph has a main idea or topic sentence and at least one sentence with supporting details comparing Navajo life in the 1600s with Navajo life today. The main idea or topic sentence may not state the comparison clearly. The supporting details may include information that is not clearly related to the main idea. The paragraph may include some errors in the use of conventions.

1 A **poor** paragraph does not have a main idea or topic sentence, or it does not have supporting details. The paragraph does not accurately compare and contrast Navajo life of the 1600s and today.

0 An **unscorable** paragraph is incomplete or has nothing to do with Navajo life.

Performance Assessment

Chapter 10: Writing a Song

Goal
The student will write a second verse for "The Texas Cowboy."

Suggestions:
1. Reread the Many Voices on page 323 and have students discuss what a second verse of the song might be about.
2. Model the process by bringing in and sharing some songs about cowboys.

Portfolio Opportunities
Have students read their songs aloud to their partners and write a sentence describing what they like best about the partner's song. Then have students display their songs, with pictures of cowboys, or place them in their portfolios with partners' comments included.

SCORING RUBRIC

4 An **excellent** second verse for "The Texas Cowboy" uses effective language to create strong visual images of cowboy life and describes typical activities of cowboys (such as line riding, camping under the stars, going on a cattle drive, branding calves). It uses the same rhythm and rhyme scheme as the first verse of the song, and it fits the same mood of longing for a distant home. The verse is written with correct use of conventions (grammar, punctuation, capitalization, and spelling).

3 A **good** second verse for "The Texas Cowboy" describes images of cowboy life and typical activities of cowboys. It uses the same rhythm and rhyme scheme as the first verse of the song, and it fits the same mood of longing for a distant home. The verse is written with generally correct use of conventions.

2 A **fair** second verse for "The Texas Cowboy" describes images of cowboy life and typical activities of cowboys. It uses the same rhyme scheme as the first verse of the song, but it may not have the same rhythm or fit the same mood of longing for a distant home. The verse may include some errors in the use of conventions.

1 A **poor** verse has no visual images or does not describe the life of a cowboy.

0 An **unscorable** verse is incomplete or is not written as a verse.

Performance Assessment

Unit 5 Review Project: Make a Southwest Wheel

Goal
The student will demonstrate knowledge of the Southwest region by making a "wheel" of questions and answers.

Suggestions:
1. Have students review Chapter 9 and discuss facts about the Southwest.
2. Model the process by listing several example questions and answers about the local community.

Portfolio Opportunities
Have students exchange wheels with partners and evaluate the wheels by using the questions on the peer assessment checklist. Then have students display their wheels and place the peer assessments in their portfolios.

SCORING RUBRIC

4 An **excellent** wheel has five well-written questions that focus on specific facts about the Southwest and five specific, accurate answers to the questions. All five questions represent important facts about different aspects of the Southwest. For example, the questions might focus on natural resources in the Southwest, types of businesses or industry, products made or grown in the Southwest, natural features or attractions of the region (such as the Grand Canyon), population centers, and climate. The text is written with correct use of conventions (grammar, punctuation, capitalization, and spelling).

3 A **good** wheel has four well-written questions that focus on specific facts about the Southwest and four specific, accurate answers to the questions. All four questions represent important facts about different aspects of the Southwest, and the wheel may include a fifth question that is not important or not appropriate or one answer that is not accurate. The text is written with generally correct use of conventions.

2 A **fair** wheel has three well-written questions that focus on specific facts about the Southwest and three specific, accurate answers to the questions. All three questions represent important facts about different aspects of the Southwest, and the wheel may include one or two other questions that are not important or not appropriate or one or two answers that are not accurate. The text may include some errors in the use of conventions.

1 A **poor** wheel has only one or two important questions, or it presents inaccurate information about the Southwest.

0 An **unscorable** project is incomplete, is not presented as a wheel, or has nothing to do with the Southwest.

Performance Assessment

Chapter 11: Writing a Comparison

Goal
The student will compare the environments of the Central Valley of California and the Amazon rain forest.

Suggestions:
1. Review Lesson 1 and the Global Connections lesson in the chapter and have students discuss how the environments in the Central Valley of California and the Amazon rain forest are alike and how they are different.
2. Model the process by making a comparison/contrast chart or by reading aloud a comparison/contrast paragraph on a different subject.

Portfolio Opportunities
Have students evaluate their own paragraphs by completing self-assessment checklists. Then have students collect their paragraphs in a notebook or place them in their portfolios with their self-assessments.

SCORING RUBRIC

4 An **excellent** comparison has a main idea or topic sentence and three or more sentences with supporting details. The main idea or topic sentence clearly states a comparison of the environments in the Central Valley of California and in the Amazon rain forest. The rest of the paragraph gives at least two comparisons and two contrasts clearly identified as "alike" or "different." For example, the Central Valley of California is flat and has fertile soil, it has a warm climate, and it has two rivers flowing through it; but it is a dry area. Little rain falls in the summer, so the valley has been irrigated to bring water to farmland. The Amazon rain forest is hot, rainy, and humid; it has fertile soil; and it has a major river flowing through it; but it is covered with an extremely thick growth of trees and other plants. Farmers have cut down enormous numbers of trees to clear land for farming. The paragraph is written with correct use of conventions (grammar, punctuation, capitalization, and spelling).

3 A **good** comparison has a main idea or topic sentence and two sentences with supporting details. The main idea or topic sentence clearly states a comparison. The rest of the paragraph gives at least one comparison and one contrast clearly identified as "alike" or "different." The paragraph is written with generally correct use of conventions.

2 A **fair** comparison has a main idea or topic sentence and at least one sentence with supporting details comparing the two environments. The main idea or topic sentence may not state the comparison clearly. The supporting details may include information that is not clearly related to the main idea. The paragraph may include some errors in the use of conventions.

1 A **poor** comparison does not have a main idea or topic sentence, or it does not have supporting details. The paragraph does not accurately compare and contrast the two environments.

0 An **unscorable** comparison is incomplete or has nothing to do with the two environments.

Performance Assessment

Chapter 11: Writing an Interview

Goal
The student writes an interview with Kim Duffy.

Suggestions:
1. Review the information on Kim Duffy in Lesson 3 and discuss the kinds of questions one might ask her about her life and what she does.
2. Model the process by having students ask you questions about what you do.

Portfolio Opportunities
Have students evaluate their own interviews by using them to role-play with partners and discussing what is good about them and what might be improved. Then have students share their interviews with the class and place the interviews in their portfolios.

SCORING RUBRIC

4 An **excellent** interview has three well-written questions and a specific response to each question. The questions are easy to understand, are specific to Kim Duffy's life as a logger in the West, lead to informative responses, and are presented in a logical sequence. At least one of the questions focuses on how or why logging has changed in the past twenty years. The responses are appropriate to the questions and provide accurate information about Duffy. The text is written with correct use of conventions (grammar, punctuation, capitalization, and spelling).

3 A **good** interview has three well-written questions and a specific response to each question. The questions are specific to Duffy, lead to informative responses, and are presented in a logical sequence. At least one of the questions focuses on how or why logging has changed in the past twenty years. The responses are appropriate to the questions and provide accurate information about Duffy, although they may not be as complete as they could be. The text is written with generally correct use of conventions.

2 A **fair** interview has two well-written questions and a specific response to each question. The interview may include other questions that are not appropriate or are not well written, and it may include some inaccurate information in the responses. The text may include some errors in the use of conventions.

1 A **poor** interview does not have clear, focused questions and does not lead to informative responses.

0 An **unscorable** interview is unreadable, is not written as an interview, or does not have anything to do with Kim Duffy.

Performance Assessment

Chapter 11: Writing a List

Goal
The student makes a list of "treasures" that come from the rain forest and their uses.

Suggestions:
1. Review the Global Connections lesson in the chapter and have students discuss the kinds of treasures that come from the rain forest.
2. Model the process by making a list of products that are grown or made in your area and what they are used for.

Portfolio Opportunities
Have students exchange lists with partners and evaluate the lists by completing peer assessment checklists. Then have students display their lists on a bulletin board or place them in their portfolios with the peer assessments.

SCORING RUBRIC

4 An **excellent** list names at least four treasures that come from the rain forest and tells what they are used for. Items on the list are numbered, bulleted, or clearly marked in some other way. Items might include mahogany, which is used to produce lumber for building; latex, which is used to make rubber; nuts and fruit, which are sources of food; tropical plants, which are used to make medicines and insect repellents. The text is written with correct use of conventions (grammar, punctuation, capitalization, and spelling).

3 A **good** list names three treasures that come from the rain forest and tells what they are used for. Items on the list are numbered, bulleted, or clearly marked in some other way. The text is written with generally correct use of conventions.

2 A **fair** list names two treasures that come from the rain forest and tells what they are used for, although the explanations may not be complete. Items on the list may not be clearly delineated. The text may include some errors in the use of conventions.

1 A **poor** list does not name a treasure that comes from the rain forest, it names treasures but does not explain their uses, or the explanations are inaccurate.

0 An **unscorable** list is incomplete or has nothing to do with treasures from the rain forest.

Performance Assessment

Chapter 12: Writing a Summary

Goal
The student describes the women's suffrage movement by writing a summary.

Suggestions:
1. Review Lesson 3 and have students determine the most important pieces of information to include in a summary.
2. Model the process by writing and/or reading aloud a paragraph describing another event or movement.

Portfolio Opportunities
Have students exchange summaries with their partners and evaluate them by completing peer assessment checklists. Then have students collect their summaries in a notebook or place them in their portfolios with the peer assessment checklists.

SCORING RUBRIC

4 An **excellent** summary has a strong topic sentence and three or more detail sentences that summarize at least four important points about the women's suffrage movement. For example, the summary might include the meeting held at Seneca Falls in 1848, the names of the leaders of the movement (such as Elizabeth Cady Stanton, Lucretia Mott, and Susan B. Anthony), the Declaration of Rights and Sentiments, early victories in the West where people had started new lives and were open to new ideas, and the passage of the Nineteenth Amendment granting women the right to vote. The text is written with correct use of conventions (grammar, punctuation, capitalization, and spelling).

3 A **good** summary has a strong topic sentence and two or more detail sentences that summarize three important points about the women's suffrage movement. The text is written with generally correct use of conventions.

2 A **fair** summary has a topic sentence and two detail sentences that summarize two important points about the women's suffrage movement. The topic sentence may not be clear, and some of the details may not represent the most important information from the lesson. The text may include some errors in the use of conventions.

1 A **poor** summary does not have a topic sentence, it does not describe the women's suffrage movement, or it presents inaccurate information.

0 An **unscorable** summary is incomplete or is not related to the women's suffrage movement.

Performance Assessment

Chapter 12: Writing an Article

Goal
The student will write a news article about the history of Hawaii from 1810 to 1959.

Suggestions:
1. Review pages 374–375 in the chapter and have students identify the most important events in Hawaii's history.
2. Model the process by bringing in and sharing a news article on the history of a state or a newly developing country.

Portfolio Opportunities
Have students work in small groups to present their articles and complete peer assessment checklists to evaluate one another's work. Then have students place their articles in their portfolios with the peer assessment checklists.

SCORING RUBRIC

4 An **excellent** article gives factual information and describes at least four events in the history of Hawaii between 1810 and 1959. It presents the information in a logical order with correct use of conventions (grammar, punctuation, capitalization, and spelling). Events might include the founding of the Kingdom of Hawaii by King Kamehameha in 1810, the arrival of James Cook, the arrival of traders looking for sandalwood, the arrival of whalers, the purchase of land and building of sugarcane and pineapple plantations, the arrival of immigrant workers for the plantations, the ascension of Queen Liliuokalani in 1891 and her overthrow by a group of business leaders in 1893, the kingdom's becoming a territory of the United States in 1898, and its achieving statehood in 1959.

3 A **good** article gives factual information and describes three major events in the history of Hawaii between 1810 and 1959. It presents the information in a logical order with generally correct use of conventions.

2 A **fair** article gives factual information and describes two major events in the history of Hawaii between 1810 and 1959. The information may not be presented in a logical order. The text may include some errors in the use of conventions.

1 A **poor** article does not give specific information about Hawaii's history or presents inaccurate information.

0 An **unscorable** article is unreadable or has nothing to do with Hawaii's history.

Performance Assessment

Chapter 12: Writing an Explanation

Goal
The student will explain how "black gold" and gold are alike and how they are different by writing a paragraph.

Suggestions:
1. Review Lesson 3 and have students discuss how "black gold" (petroleum) is similar to and different from gold.
2. Model the process by making a comparison/contrast chart or by reading aloud a comparison/contrast paragraph on a different subject.

Portfolio Opportunities
Have students exchange paragraphs with their partners and evaluate the paragraphs by completing peer assessment checklists. Then have students collect their paragraphs in a notebook or place them in their portfolios with the peer assessments.

SCORING RUBRIC

4 An **excellent** paragraph has a main idea or topic sentence and three or more sentences with supporting details. The main idea or topic sentence clearly states a comparison of "black gold" and gold. The rest of the paragraph gives at least two comparisons and two contrasts clearly identified as "alike" or "different." For example, "black gold" and gold are alike in that they are both taken out of the ground, they both exist in a limited supply and cannot be replaced, they are both very valuable, and they have both caused rapid growth in the West and Southwest (in the "boom towns" in Texas and Oklahoma and in the gold rushes in California and the Yukon). They are different in how they are extracted from the earth and how they are used. Petroleum and petrochemicals are necessities for our current way of life, but gold is a luxury and a source of wealth. The paragraph is written with correct use of conventions (grammar, punctuation, capitalization, and spelling).

3 A **good** paragraph has a main idea or topic sentence and two sentences with supporting details. The main idea or topic sentence clearly states a comparison. The rest of the paragraph gives at least one comparison and one contrast clearly identified as "alike" or "different." The paragraph is written with generally correct use of conventions.

2 A **fair** paragraph has a main idea or topic sentence and at least one sentence with supporting details explaining how "black gold" and gold are alike and different. The main idea or topic sentence may not state the comparison clearly. The supporting details may include information that is not clearly related to the main idea. The paragraph may include some errors in the use of conventions.

1 A **poor** paragraph does not have a main idea or topic sentence, or it does not have supporting details. The paragraph does not accurately compare and contrast "black gold" and gold.

0 An **unscorable** paragraph is incomplete or has nothing to do with "black gold" and gold.

Performance Assessment

Unit 6 Review Project: Make a Postcard Collection

Goal
The student will describe four national parks in the western United States by making postcards.

Suggestions:
1. Have students brainstorm or research a list of national parks in the western United States and discuss the kinds of information that should be included on a postcard describing a national park.
2. Model the process by making a postcard about a national park near your community.

Portfolio Opportunities
Have students exchange postcards with partners and evaluate the postcards by using the questions on the peer assessment checklist. Then have students display their postcards (or send them to friends) and place the peer assessments in their portfolios.

SCORING RUBRIC

4 An **excellent** postcard collection has four postcards with factual information about four different national parks in the western United States. Each postcard has at least four facts on one side and an appropriate picture or decoration on the other side. Factual information might describe the park's climate, wildlife, history, and places of interest. The text is written with correct use of conventions (grammar, punctuation, capitalization, and spelling).

3 A **good** postcard collection has four postcards with factual information about four different national parks in the western United States. Each postcard has three facts on one side and an appropriate picture or decoration on the other side. The text is written with generally correct use of conventions.

2 A **fair** postcard collection has four postcards with factual information about four different national parks in the western United States. Each postcard has one or two facts on one side and an appropriate picture of some kind on the other side. The text may include some errors in the use of conventions.

1 A **poor** postcard collection has fewer than four postcards, one or no pieces of factual information about each park, or inaccurate information about the parks.

0 An **unscorable** postcard collection is incomplete or does not relate to national parks in the western United States.

the White Stripes

2	Dead Leaves and the Dirty Ground
7	Hotel Yorba
10	I'm Finding It Harder to Be a Gentleman
14	Fell in Love with a Girl
18	Expecting
21	Little Room
22	The Union Forever
26	The Same Boy You've Always Known
30	We're Going to Be Friends
33	Offend in Every Way
36	I Think I Smell a Rat
39	Aluminum
41	I Can't Wait
45	Now Mary
49	I Can Learn
52	This Protector
54	*Guitar Notation Legend*

Photography by Patrick Pantano

ISBN 1-57560-627-5

Copyright © 2003 Cherry Lane Music Company
International Copyright Secured   All Rights Reserved

The music, text, design and graphics in this publication are protected by copyright law.
Any duplication or transmission, by any means, electronic, mechanical, photocopying, recording or otherwise, is an infringement of copyright.

Visit our website at www.cherrylane.com

DEAD LEAVES AND THE DIRTY GROUND

Words and Music by
Jack White

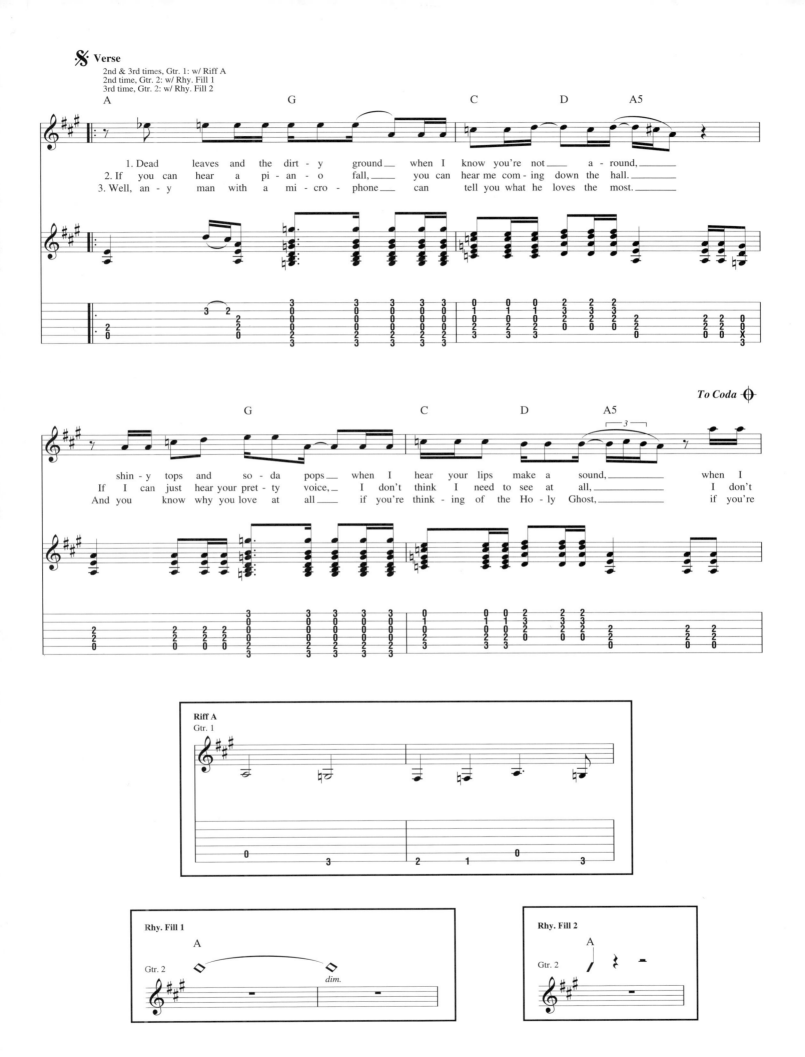

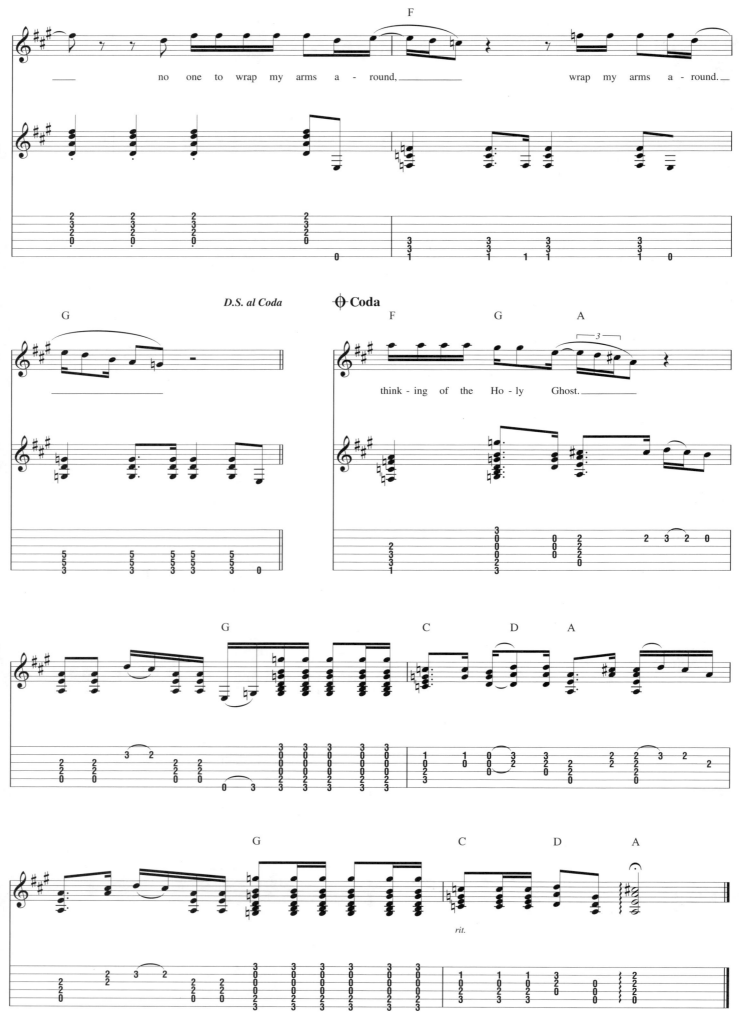

HOTEL YORBA

Words and Music by
Jack White

I'M FINDING IT HARDER TO BE A GENTLEMAN

Words and Music by
Jack White

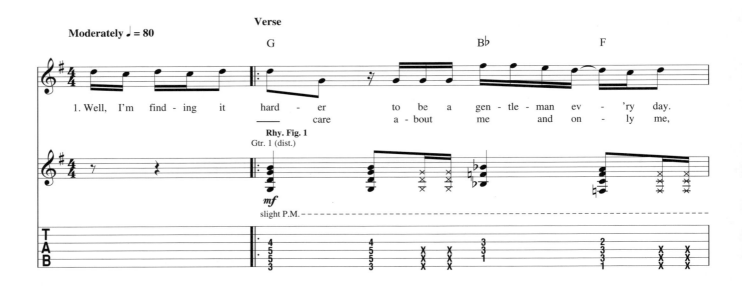

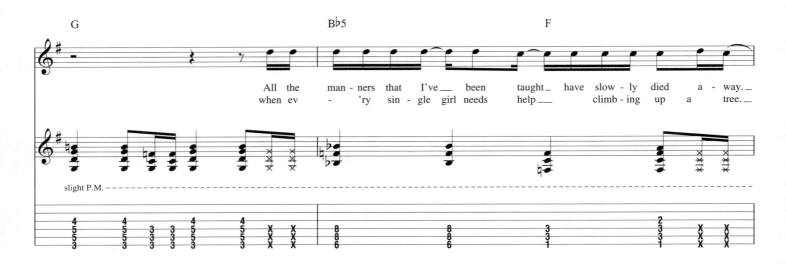

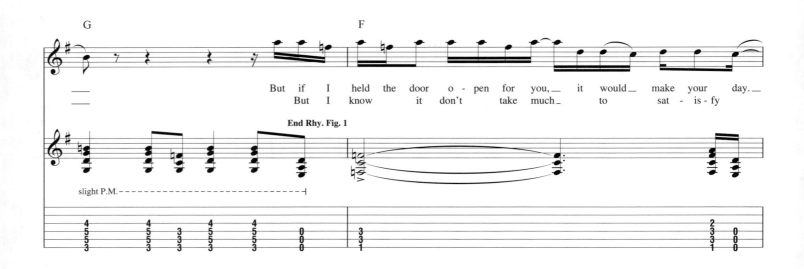

Copyright © 2001 Peppermint Stripe Music (BMI)
All Rights Reserved   Used by Permission

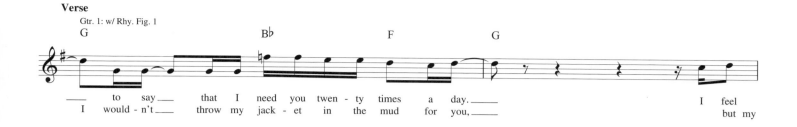
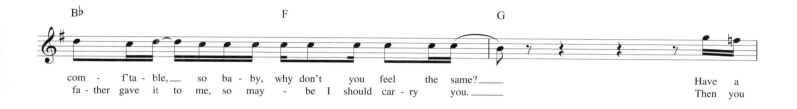
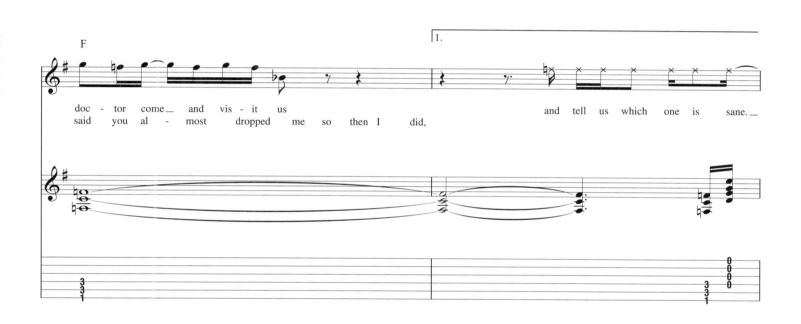
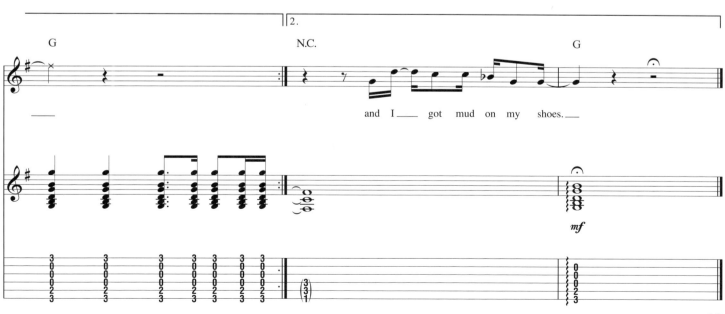

13

FELL IN LOVE WITH A GIRL

Words and Music by
Jack White

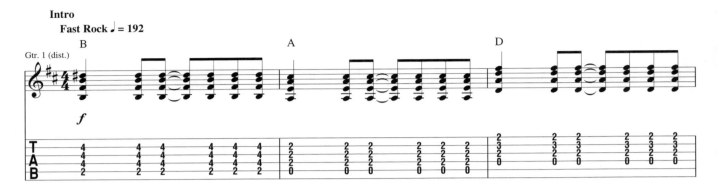
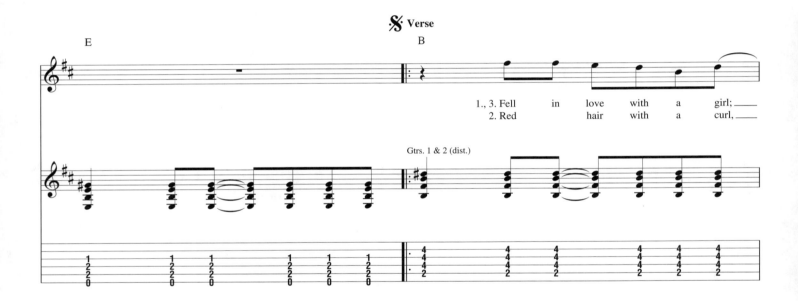

Copyright © 2001 Peppermint Stripe Music (BMI)
All Rights Reserved   Used by Permission

LITTLE ROOM

Words and Music by
Jack White

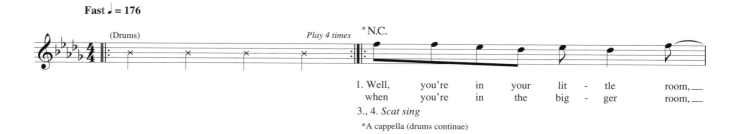

Copyright © 2001 Peppermint Stripe Music (BMI)
All Rights Reserved   Used by Permission

THE UNION FOREVER

Words and Music by
Jack White and Pepe Guizar

Copyright © 2001, 2002 Peppermint Stripe Music (BMI) and Peer International Corporation
All Rights Reserved   Used by Permission

THE SAME BOY YOU'VE ALWAYS KNOWN

Words and Music by
Jack White

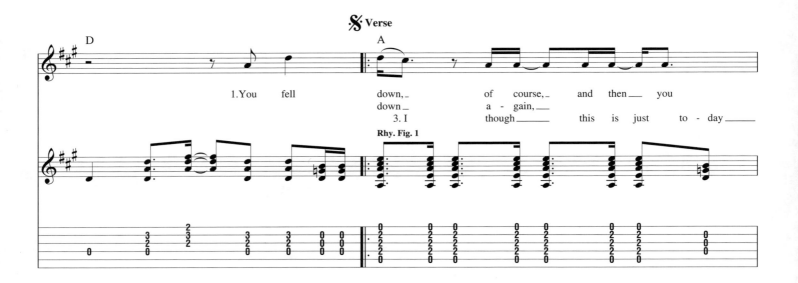

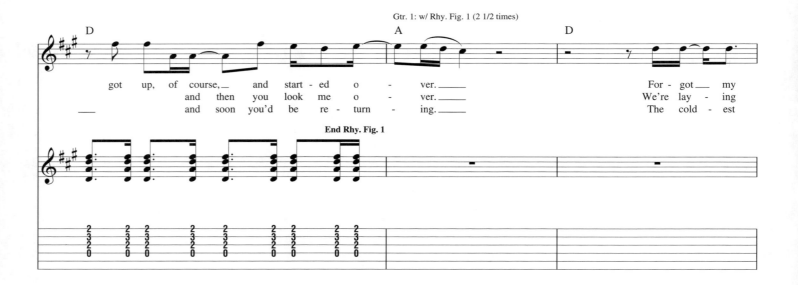

Copyright © 2001 Peppermint Stripe Music (BMI)
All Rights Reserved   Used by Permission

WE'RE GOING TO BE FRIENDS

Words and Music by
Jack White

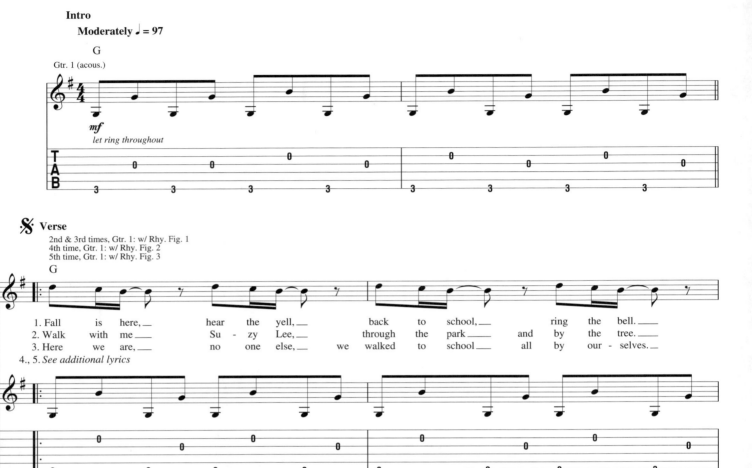

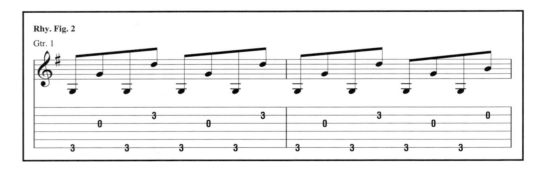

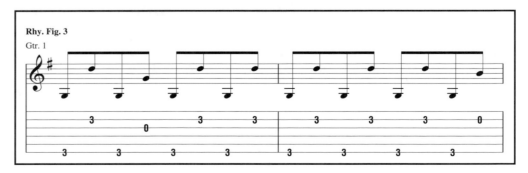

Copyright © 2001 Peppermint Stripe Music (BMI)
All Rights Reserved Used by Permission

Additional Lyrics

4. Numbers, letters, learn to spell.
   Nouns and books and show-and-tell.
   Playtime we will throw the ball,
   Back to class, through the hall.
   Teacher marks our height against the wall,
   Teacher marks our height against the wall. *(To Bridge)*

5. Tonight I'll dream while I'm in bed,
   When silly thoughts go through my head,
   About the bugs and alphabet.
   And when I wake tomorrow I'll bet that
   You and I will walk together again.
   I can tell that we are gonna be friends. *(To Coda)*

OFFEND IN EVERY WAY

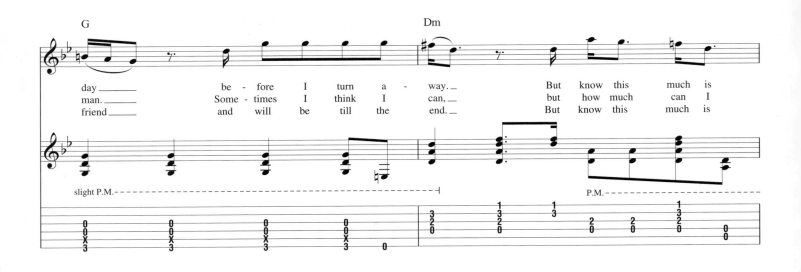

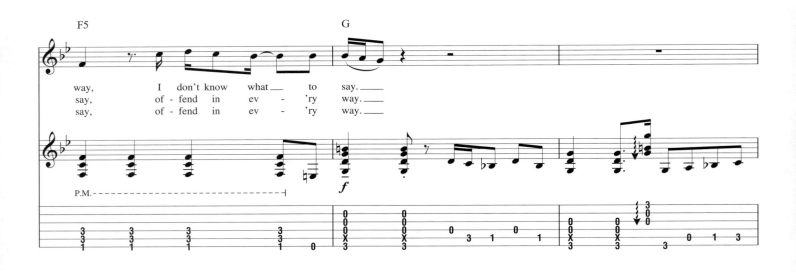
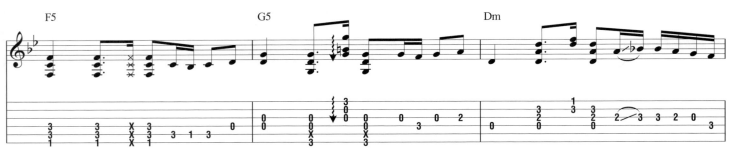

I THINK I SMELL A RAT

Words and Music by
Jack White

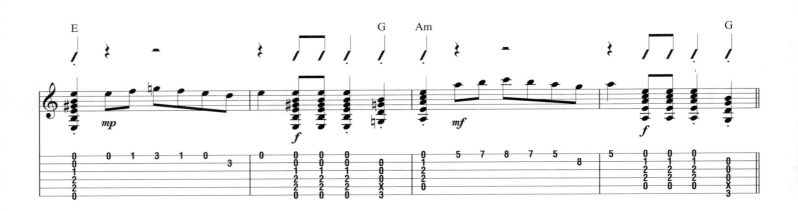

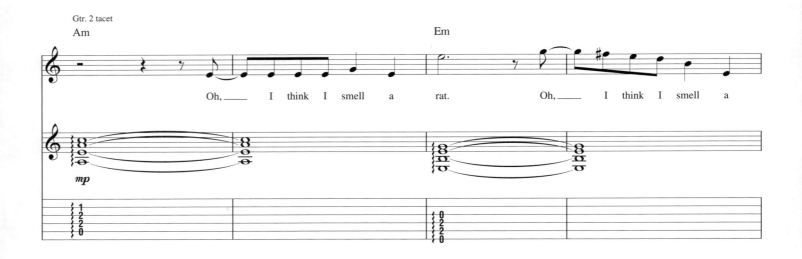

ALUMINUM

Words and Music by
Jack White

Intro
Moderately ♩ = 62

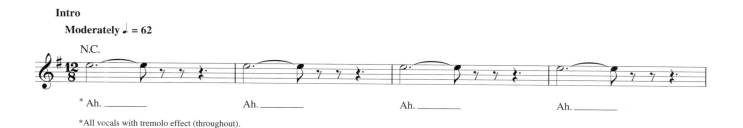

* Ah.   Ah.   Ah.   Ah.

*All vocals with tremolo effect (throughout).

*Gtr. 1 (dist.)

*w/ heavy dist. & random fdbk. throughout.

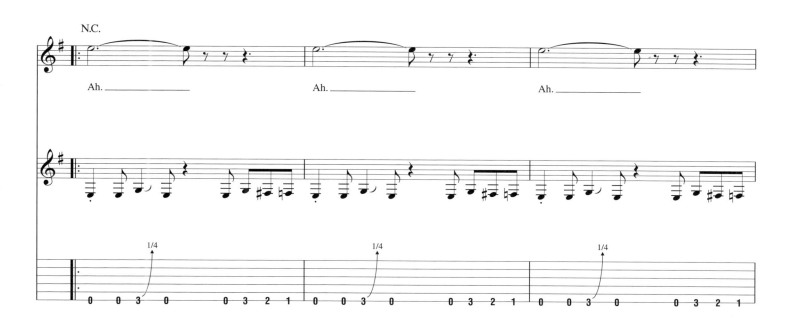

Ah.   Ah.   Ah.

Copyright © 2001 Peppermint Stripe Music (BMI)
All Rights Reserved   Used by Permission

I CAN'T WAIT

Words and Music by Jack White

Copyright © 2001 Peppermint Stripe Music (BMI)
All Rights Reserved   Used by Permission

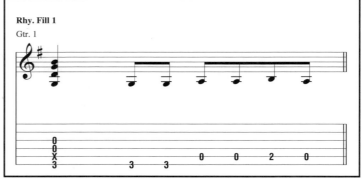

I CAN LEARN

Words and Music by Jack White

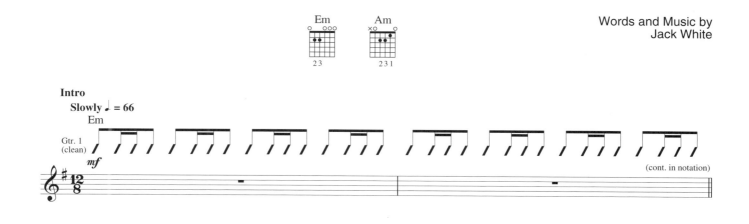

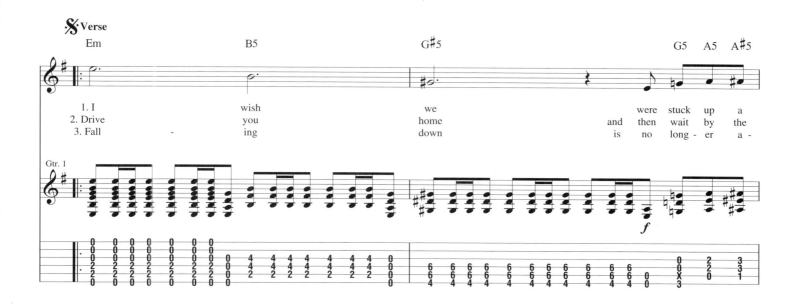

Copyright © 2001 Peppermint Stripe Music (BMI)
All Rights Reserved   Used by Permission

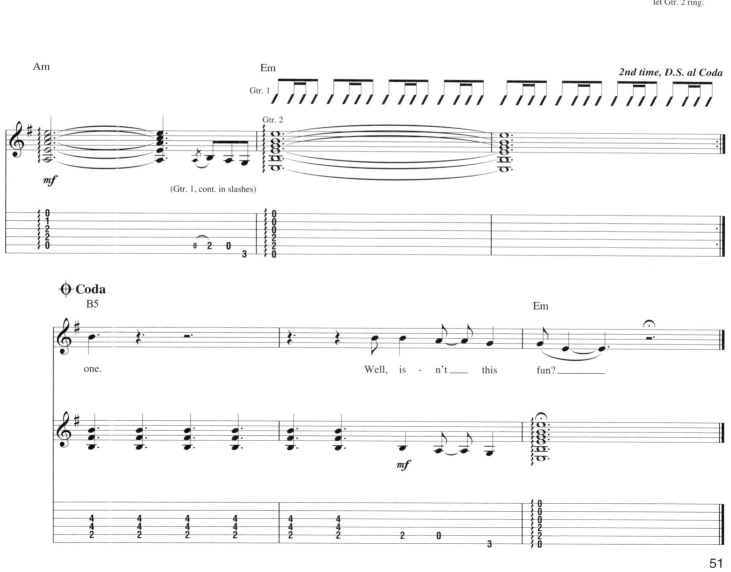

THIS PROTECTOR

Words and Music by
Jack White

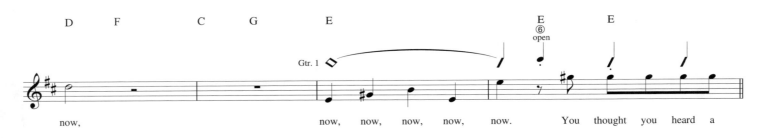

Copyright © 2001 Peppemint Stripe Music (BMI)
All Rights Reserved   Used by Permission

Guitar Notation Legend

Guitar Music can be notated three different ways: on a *musical staff*, in *tablature*, and in *rhythm slashes*.

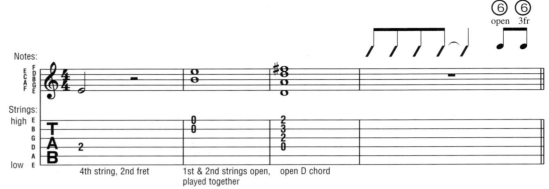

RHYTHM SLASHES are written above the staff. Strum chords in the rhythm indicated. Use the chord diagrams found at the top of the first page of the transcription for the appropriate chord voicings. Round noteheads indicate single notes.

THE MUSICAL STAFF shows pitches and rhythms and is divided by bar lines into measures. Pitches are named after the first seven letters of the alphabet.

TABLATURE graphically represents the guitar fingerboard. Each horizontal line represents a string, and each number represents a fret.

HALF-STEP BEND: Strike the note and bend up 1/2 step.

WHOLE-STEP BEND: Strike the note and bend up one step.

GRACE NOTE BEND: Strike the note and immediately bend up as indicated.

SLIGHT (MICROTONE) BEND: Strike the note and bend up 1/4 step.

BEND AND RELEASE: Strike the note and bend up as indicated, then release back to the original note. Only the first note is struck.

PRE-BEND: Bend the note as indicated, then strike it.

VIBRATO: The string is vibrated by rapidly bending and releasing the note with the fretting hand.

WIDE VIBRATO: The pitch is varied to a greater degree by vibrating with the fretting hand.

HAMMER-ON: Strike the first (lower) note with one finger, then sound the higher note (on the same string) with another finger by fretting it without picking.

PULL-OFF: Place both fingers on the notes to be sounded. Strike the first note and without picking, pull the finger off to sound the second (lower) note.

LEGATO SLIDE: Strike the first note and then slide the same fret-hand finger up or down to the second note. The second note is not struck.

SHIFT SLIDE: Same as legato slide, except the second note is struck.

TRILL: Very rapidly alternate between the notes indicated by continuously hammering on and pulling off.

TAPPING: Hammer ("tap") the fret indicated with the pick-hand index or middle finger and pull off to the note fretted by the fret hand.

NATURAL HARMONIC: Strike the note while the fret-hand lightly touches the string directly over the fret indicated.

PINCH HARMONIC: The note is fretted normally and a harmonic is produced by adding the edge of the thumb or the tip of the index finger of the pick hand to the normal pick attack.

PICK SCRAPE: The edge of the pick is rubbed down (or up) the string, producing a scratchy sound.

MUFFLED STRINGS: A percussive sound is produced by laying the fret hand across the string(s) without depressing, and striking them with the pick hand.

PALM MUTING: The note is partially muted by the pick hand lightly touching the string(s) just before the bridge.

RAKE: Drag the pick across the strings indicated with a single motion.

TREMOLO PICKING: The note is picked as rapidly and continuously as possible.

VIBRATO BAR DIVE AND RETURN: The pitch of the note or chord is dropped a specified number of steps (in rhythm) then returned to the original pitch.

VIBRATO BAR SCOOP: Depress the bar just before striking the note, then quickly release the bar.

VIBRATO BAR DIP: Strike the note and then immediately drop a specified number of steps, then release back to the original pitch.

CHERRY LANE MUSIC COMPANY
6 East 32nd Street, New York, NY 10016

Quality in Printed Music

The Magazine You Can Play

Visit the Guitar One web site at **www.guitarone.com**

ACOUSTIC INSTRUMENTALISTS
Over 15 transcriptions from legendary artists such as Leo Kottke, John Fahey, Jorma Kaukonen, Chet Atkins, Adrian Legg, Jeff Beck, and more.

02500399 Play-It-Like-It-Is Guitar............................$9.95

THE BEST BASS LINES
24 super songs: Bohemian Rhapsody • Celebrity Skin • Crash Into Me • Crazy Train • Glycerine • Money • November Rain • Smoke on the Water • Sweet Child O' Mine • What Would You Say • You're My Flavor • and more.
02500311 Play-It-Like-It-Is Bass $14.95

BLUES TAB
14 songs: Boom Boom • Cold Shot • Hide Away • I Can't Quit You Baby • I'm Your Hoochie Coochie Man • In 2 Deep • It Hurts Me Too • Talk to Your Daughter • The Thrill Is Gone • and more.
02500410 Play-It-Like-It-Is Guitar..........................$14.95

CLASSIC ROCK TAB
15 rock hits: Cat Scratch Fever • Crazy Train • Day Tripper • Hey Joe • Hot Blooded • Start Me Up • We Will Rock You • You Really Got Me • and more.
02500408 Play-It-Like-It-Is Guitar..........................$14.95

MODERN ROCK TAB
15 of modern rock's best: Are You Gonna Go My Way • Denial • Hanging by a Moment • I Did It • My Hero • Nobody's Real • Rock the Party (Off the Hook) • Shock the Monkey • Slide • Spit It Out • and more.
02500409 Play-It-Like-It-Is Guitar..........................$14.95

SIGNATURE SONGS
21 artists' trademark hits: Crazy Train (Ozzy Osbourne) • My Generation (The Who) • Smooth (Santana) • Sunshine of Your Love (Cream) • Walk This Way (Aerosmith) • Welcome to the Jungle (Guns N' Roses) • What Would You Say (Dave Matthews Band) • and more.
02500303 Play-It-Like-It-Is Guitar..........................$16.95

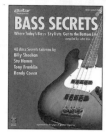

BASS SECRETS
WHERE TODAY'S BASS STYLISTS GET TO THE BOTTOM LINE
compiled by John Stix
Bass Secrets brings together 48 columns highlighting specific topics – ranging from the technical to the philosophical – from masters such as Stu Hamm, Randy Coven, Tony Franklin and Billy Sheehan. They cover topics including tapping, walking bass lines, soloing, hand positions, harmonics and more. Clearly illustrated with musical examples.
02500100 ....$12.95

CLASSICS ILLUSTRATED
WHERE BACH MEETS ROCK
by Robert Phillips
Classics Illustrated is designed to demonstrate for readers and players the links between rock and classical music. Each of the 30 columns from *Guitar* highlights one musical concept and provides clear examples in both styles of music. This cool book lets you study moving bass lines over stationary chords in the music of Bach and Guns N' Roses, learn the similarities between "Leyenda" and "Diary of a Madman," and much more!
02500101 ....$9.95

GUITAR SECRETS
WHERE ROCK'S GUITAR MASTERS SHARE THEIR TRICKS, TIPS & TECHNIQUES
compiled by John Stix
This unique and informative compilation features 42 columns culled from *Guitar* magazine. Readers will discover dozens of techniques and playing tips, and gain practical advice and words of wisdom from guitar masters.
02500099 ....$10.95

IN THE LISTENING ROOM
WHERE ARTISTS CRITIQUE THE MUSIC OF THEIR PEERS
compiled by John Stix
A compilation of 75 columns from *Guitar* magazine, *In the Listening Room* provides a unique opportunity for readers to hear major recording artists remark on the music of their peers. These artists were given no information about what they would hear, and their comments often tell as much about themselves as they do about the music they listened to. Includes candid critiques by music legends like Aerosmith, Jeff Beck, Jack Bruce, Dimebag Darrell, Buddy Guy, Kirk Hammett, Eric Johnson, John McLaughlin, Dave Navarro, Carlos Santana, Joe Satriani, Stevie Ray Vaughan, and many others.
02500097 ....$14.95

EXCLUSIVELY DISTRIBUTED BY

7777 W. BLUEMOUND RD. P.O. BOX 13819 MILWAUKEE, WI 53213

Visit Cherry Lane online at **www.cherrylane.com**

REFERENCE/INSTRUCTION

LEGENDS OF LEAD GUITAR
THE BEST OF INTERVIEWS: 1995-2000
This is a fascinating compilation of interviews with today's greatest guitarists! From deeply rooted blues giants to the most fearless pioneers, legendary players reveal how they achieve their extraordinary craft.
02500329 ....$14.95

LESSON LAB
This exceptional book/CD pack features more than 20 in-depth lessons. Tackle in detail a variety of pertinent music- and guitar-related subjects, such as scales, chords, theory, guitar technique, songwriting, and much more!
02500330 Book/CD Pack.......................................$19.95

NOISE & FEEDBACK
THE BEST OF 1995-2000: YOUR QUESTIONS ANSWERED
If you ever wanted to know about a specific guitar lick, trick, technique or effect, this book/CD pack is for you! It features over 70 lessons on composing • computer assistance • education and career advice • equipment • technique • terminology and notation • tunings • and more.
02500328 Book/CD Pack.......................................$17.95

OPEN EARS
A JOURNEY THROUGH LIFE WITH GUITAR IN HAND
by Steve Morse
In this collection of 50 *Guitar* magazine columns from the mid-'90s on, guitarist Steve Morse sets the story straight about what being a working musician *really* means. He deals out practical advice on: playing with the band, songwriting, recording and equipment, and more, through anecdotes of his hard-knock lessons learned.
02500333 ....$10.95

SPOTLIGHT ON STYLE
THE BEST OF 1995-2000: AN EXPLORER'S GUIDE TO GUITAR
This book and CD cover 18 of the world's most popular guitar styles, including: blues guitar • classical guitar • country guitar • funk guitar • jazz guitar • Latin guitar • metal • rockabilly and more!
02500320 Book/CD Pack.......................................$19.95

STUDIO CITY
PROFESSIONAL SESSION RECORDING FOR GUITARISTS
by Carl Verheyen
In this collection of colomns from Guitar Magazine, guitarists will learn how to: exercise studio etiquette and act professionally • acquire, assemble and set up gear for sessions • use the tricks of the trade to become a studio hero • get repeat call-backs • and more.
02500195 ....$9.95

THE HOTTEST TAB SONGBOOKS AVAILABLE FOR GUITAR & BASS!

from

CHERRY LANE MUSIC COMPANY
Quality in Printed Music

Guitar Transcriptions

02500593	Best of Ryan Adams	$19.95
02500443	Alien Ant Farm – ANThology	$19.95
02501272	Bush – 16 Stone	$21.95
02500193	Bush – The Science of Things	$19.95
02500098	Coal Chamber	$19.95
02500174	Coal Chamber – Chamber Music	$19.95
02500179	Mary Chapin Carpenter – Authentic Guitar Style of	$16.95
02500132	Evolution of Fear Factory	$19.95
02500198	Best of Foreigner	$19.95
02501242	Guns N' Roses – Anthology	$24.95
02506953	Guns N' Roses – Appetite for Destruction	$22.95
02501286	Guns N' Roses Complete, Volume 1	$24.95
02501287	Guns N' Roses Complete, Volume 2	$24.95
02506211	Guns N' Roses – 5 of the Best, Vol. 1	$12.95
02506975	Guns N' Roses – GN'R Lies	$19.95
02500299	Guns N' Roses – Live Era '87-'93 Highlights	$24.95
02501193	Guns N' Roses – Use Your Illusion I	$24.95
02501194	Guns N' Roses – Use Your Illusion II	$24.95
02500458	Best of Warren Haynes	$19.95
02500387	Best of Heart	$19.95
02500007	Hole – Celebrity Skin	$19.95
02501260	Hole – Live Through This	$19.95
02500516	Jimmy Eat World	$19.95
02500554	Jack Johnson – Brushfire Fairytales	$19.95
02500380	Lenny Kravitz – Greatest Hits	$19.95
02500469	Lenny Kravitz – Lenny	$19.95
02500024	Best of Lenny Kravitz	$19.95
02500375	Lifehouse – No Name Face	$19.95
02500558	Lifehouse – Stanley Climbfall	$19.95
02500362	Best of Little Feat	$19.95
02501259	Machine Head – Burn My Eyes	$19.95
02500173	Machine Head – The Burning Red	$19.95
02500305	Best of The Marshall Tucker Band	$19.95
02501357	Dave Matthews Band – Before These Crowded Streets	$19.95
02500553	Dave Matthews Band – Busted Stuff	$22.95
02501279	Dave Matthews Band – Crash	$19.95
02500389	Dave Matthews Band – Everyday	$19.95
02500488	Dave Matthews Band – Live in Chicago 12/19/98 at the United Center, Vol. 1	$19.95
02500489	Dave Matthews Band – Live in Chicago 12/19/98 at the United Center, Vol. 2	$19.95
02501266	Dave Matthews Band – Under the Table and Dreaming	$19.95
02500131	Dave Matthews/Tim Reynolds – Live at Luther College, Vol. 1	$19.95
02500611	Dave Matthews/Tim Reynolds – Live at Luther College, Vol. 2	$19.95
02500529	John Mayer – Room for Squares	$19.95
02506965	Metallica – ...And Justice for All	$22.95
02506210	Metallica – 5 of the Best/Vol.1	$12.95
02506235	Metallica – 5 of the Best/Vol. 2	$12.95
02500070	Metallica – Garage, Inc.	$24.95
02507018	Metallica – Kill 'Em All	$19.95
02501232	Metallica – Live: Binge & Purge	$19.95
02501275	Metallica – Load	$24.95
02507920	Metallica – Master of Puppets	$19.95
02501195	Metallica – Metallica	$22.95
02501297	Metallica – ReLoad	$24.95
02507019	Metallica – Ride the Lightning	$19.95
02500279	Metallica – S&M Highlights	$24.95
02500577	Molly Hatchet – 5 of the Best	$9.95
02501353	Best of Steve Morse	$19.95
02500448	Best of Ted Nugent	$19.95
02500348	Ozzy Osbourne – Blizzard of Ozz	$19.95
02501277	Ozzy Osbourne – Diary of a Madman	$19.95
02509973	Ozzy Osbourne – Songbook	$24.95
02507904	Ozzy Osbourne/Randy Rhoads Tribute	$22.95
02500316	Papa Roach – Infest	$19.95
02500545	Papa Roach – Lovehatetragedy	$19.95
02500194	Powerman 5000 – Tonight the Stars Revolt!	$17.95
02500025	Primus Anthology – A-N (Guitar/Bass)	$19.95
02500091	Primus Anthology – O-Z (Guitar/Bass)	$19.95
02500468	Primus – Sailing the Seas of Cheese	$19.95
02500508	Bonnie Raitt – Silver Lining	$19.95
02501268	Joe Satriani	$22.95
02501299	Joe Satriani – Crystal Planet	$24.95
02500306	Joe Satriani – Engines of Creation	$22.95
02501205	Joe Satriani – The Extremist	$22.95
02507029	Joe Satriani – Flying in a Blue Dream	$22.95
02507074	Joe Satriani – Not of This Earth	$19.95
02500544	Joe Satriani – Strange Beautiful Music	$19.95
02506959	Joe Satriani – Surfing with the Alien	$19.95
02501226	Joe Satriani – Time Machine 1	$19.95
02500560	Joe Satriani Anthology	$24.95
02501255	Best of Joe Satriani	$19.95
02500088	Sepultura – Against	$19.95
02501239	Sepultura – Arise	$19.95
02501240	Sepultura – Beneath the Remains	$19.95
02501238	Sepultura – Chaos A.D.	$19.95
02500188	Best of the Brian Setzer Orchestra	$19.95
02500177	Sevendust	$19.95
02500176	Sevendust – Home	$19.95
02500090	Soulfly	$19.95
02501230	Soundgarden – Superunknown	$19.95
02501250	Best of Soundgarden	$19.95
02500168	Steely Dan's Greatest Songs	$19.95
02500167	Best of Steely Dan for Guitar	$19.95
02501263	Tesla – Time's Making Changes	$19.95
02500583	The White Stripes – White Blood Cells	$19.95
02500431	Best of Johnny Winter	$19.95
02500199	Best of Zakk Wylde	$22.95
02500517	WWE – Forceable Entry	$19.95
02500104	WWF: The Music, Vol.3	$19.95

Bass Transcriptions

02500008	Best of Bush	$16.95
02505920	Bush – 16 Stone	$19.95
02506966	Guns N' Roses – Appetite for Destruction	$19.95
02500504	Best of Guns N' Roses for Bass	$14.95
02500013	Best of The Dave Matthews Band	$17.95
02505911	Metallica – Metallica	$19.95
02506982	Metallica – ...And Justice for All	$19.95
02500075	Metallica – Garage, Inc.	$24.95
02507039	Metallica – Kill 'Em All	$19.95
02505919	Metallica – Load	$19.95
02506961	Metallica – Master of Puppets	$19.95
02505926	Metallica – ReLoad	$21.95
02507040	Metallica – Ride the Lightning	$17.95
02500288	Metallica – S&M Highlights	$19.95
02500347	Papa Roach – Infest	$17.95
02500539	Sittin' In with Rocco Prestia of Tower of Power	$19.95
02500025	Primus Anthology – A-N (Guitar/Bass)	$19.95
02500091	Primus Anthology – O-Z (Guitar/Bass)	$19.95
02500500	Best of Joe Satriani for Bass	$14.95
02500317	Victor Wooten Songbook	$19.95

Transcribed Scores

02500361	Guns N' Roses Greatest Hits	$24.95
02500282	Lenny Kravitz – Greatest Hits	$24.95
02500496	Lenny Kravitz – Lenny	$24.95
02500424	Best of Metallica	$24.95
02500283	Joe Satriani – Greatest Hits	$24.95

FOR MORE INFORMATION, SEE YOUR LOCAL MUSIC DEALER, OR WRITE TO:

HAL•LEONARD CORPORATION
7777 W. BLUEMOUND RD. P.O. BOX 13819 MILWAUKEE, WI 53213

Prices, contents and availability subject to change without notice.

0303